Cape Cod Camino Way

Walking with a Purpose

By Peggy Jablonski

Edited by Megan Nussle
Book Design by Chloe Heidepriem
Cover, Logo, and Maps by Saraphina Churchill

First Edition: June 2021

Table of Contents

Reflections on
Cape Cod Camino Way

"The earth will always tell a story. With every step across this vast peninsula comes a stark reality that out of pain and beauty lies the true history and contributions of BIPOC. Our contributions are indelibly etched into the clay, soil and sand. It is written that if we don't speak truth the rocks will cry out. How fitting that sometimes we must simply get quiet and set out in search of what brings us to where we are today and acknowledge and celebrate our yesterdays. Every resident of Cape Cod should take the walk to gain an understanding that people of color are here, we belong here, we labored and built here. We are blessed to be standing on sacred ground and we are all in this together. I thank Peggy for doing her part in leading us in telling the story."
-Marie Younger Blackburn, CEO/President of Driven: Cape Cod's Conference for Women

"Peggy has taken action and found a creative approach to sharing what she is learning about underrepresented groups on Cape Cod. She is a role model for me and others on how to be a white ally."
-Andi Genser, former Executive Director of Women's Empowerment through Cape Area Networking (WE CAN)

"The Cape Cod Camino Way was a once in a lifetime project and an incredible thing to be a part of. To deepen my understanding of the Black Lives Matter movement was such an incredibly powerful experience. To have met such influential people and hear the amazing stories of activists and people of color was truly unforgettable. I am honored to have been a part of the Cape Cod Camino Way!"
-Lilli Feronti, High School Student, Falmouth

"Cape Cod Camino Way was a healthy outlet for anyone who walked with us as we were trying to make sense of and survive unprecedented challenges. These times, and this project, gave us a glimpse of the hardship people of color have known for decades, centuries."
-Lauren Miklavic, Dennis

"I appreciated the careful and comprehensive research that Peggy undertook which helped both enlighten and dismay me. Racial inequality and injustices right in our own 'backyard' was, while not a total surprise, affirmed by Peggy's material. We have much history—some good, some dreadful—on the Cape with European settlers, Native Americans, Portuguese and Africans, those held as slaves and later part of the Underground Railroad. Peggy brought us to actual buildings and beautiful beaches where events had occurred, giving a new perspective on the beauty and history of Cape Cod. Walking, talking and listening was a powerful 'living history' experience. I cannot wait for the next one!"
-Susan Fernald, Barnstable and Nantucket

Acknowledgments

Cape Cod Camino Way: Walking with a Purpose is a product of many forces and people coming together in 2020 to create a learning experience that continues to evolve in exciting ways. Without the Covid-19 pandemic and the "Great Pause" enabled by staying close to home, I would not have had the idea to walk the peninsula of Cape Cod to explore issues of social and racial justice. Let me start by acknowledging this silver lining of the pandemic for generating profound shifts within me and around me.

I acknowledge those who came before me on this land, the Wampanoag peoples, who cared for this sacred place for thousands of years before the white Europeans arrived, claimed the land, and forced their culture upon those already living here. I am grateful for their stories that I have only just begun to hear, and for their wisdom I am just beginning to understand.

This journal of my pilgrimage across the Cape, and the people and places I visited, is my gift to anyone exploring what it means to "become aware" of what we did not know before, what we were not taught in school or by our families about social justice. This book owes its genesis to many sponsors, partners, colleagues, friends, and family. I apologize in advance for those I don't name directly, and please know that hundreds have supported my growth and development over the years that led to the conception of the Camino Way.

A brief note about the writing and sources: to create the walks each week, I complied information from a variety of sources—websites, articles, books, songs, documents, Wikipedia, interviews, etc. I would quote directly from a source while on the walk and provide the appropriate credit. In putting together this journal, I've tried to find all the sources I referenced on the walks and either quote directly with proper citation, or rewrite the information from memory. I apologize in advance if there are places where appropriate technical/academic citations are missing. In weaving together hundreds of sources, I am narrating a journey rooted in a variety of historical viewpoints, and at times taking some liberties to make assumptions or connections to further this narrative. This is my story, from memory and recreation.

To all my friends who spent countless hours exploring issues of social justice and oppression with me, especially Licia Fields, Jennie Mignone, and Colleen Holden who read *White Fragility* with me the winter of 2020, thank you for supporting each other's learning. To Kathy Obear and the White Accountability Group colleagues who met over the course of 2020, thank you for your honesty and your challenges. To the "wise women" deans of NASPA in New England who have worked together and loved each other for decades, thank you for the Zoom support and critical feedback.

To my women's coffee hour group who met regularly through Covid, germinating many "pandemic pivots," and includes Gwynne Guzzeau, Maggie French, Andi Genser, and Kathy McNamara—thank you. You helped "birth" this project, providing thoughtful feedback and wise wisdom along the path.

To my colleagues and students at UMass Amherst, MIT, Brown, UNC Chapel Hill, Boston University, and other colleges at which I attended or worked: you are all part of my foundation, experience, and growth. I am deeply grateful to Bridgewater State University as a place where I continue to affiliate and explore complex social issues.

I am blessed with a close and open family, with members with a variety of religious, racial, ethnic, sexual orientation, ability, and other identity characteristics that make our family a rich universe of possibility. I am deeply grateful to Marie for providing logistical support on several walks, and Steve, Jillian, and Laurel for being part of the process. I thank Ken for being the family member I will always turn to, for your loving support of my crazy ideas, and sustained work to bring the Camino Way to life. To share this journey with my family means the world to me.

To the 43 people who walked part or all of the Camino Way with me (or joined us at one of the stops along the way), you provided inspiration and hope for the possibility of true change. Several people walked multiple times through heat, humidity, rain, and winds. I will treasure our treks and talks along the bike paths and backroads of the Cape. One special soul, Lauren Miklavic, walked all eight weeks with me, sustaining me through the peaks and valleys, and shaping the Camino Way in her footsteps. All the walkers were a blessing!

To all the staff and volunteers of the museums, historical societies, libraries, churches, arts organizations, and tourism offices who assisted with information, facts, special programs, and other resources, I greatly appreciate your willingness to go the extra mile during the pandemic.

To those 250 people who followed the journey on the Facebook page, or the countless others who inquired about the Camino Way Project and the learning taking place, thank you for being open to raising your awareness and committing to a future of inclusion and equity for all.

To the Camino Way Team of 2020: Ken Abert, Chloe Heidepriem, Lilli Feronti, Patricia Pinto Da Silva (the fabulous coach), thank you for your administrative and social media support. And thanks to the Camino Team 2021 who brought this book to life, built a new website, organized walks for the summer of 2021, and much more to come: Dani Davis, Megan Nussle, Saraphina Churchill, Beth O'Rourke, Ken, and Chloe. Special thanks to Megan for her skill as an editor! This book would never see the light of day without your talent.

And to all who engage in the work of eradicating injustice, I dedicate this book and my future walks on the Cape Cod Camino Way to you. Keep walking, keep learning!

Peggy Jablonski
Spring, 2021

Clarification of Terms

Anti-racism: a form of action against racial hatred, bias, systemic racism, and the oppression of specific groups. Anti-racism is usually structured around conscious efforts and deliberate actions to provide equal opportunities for all people on an individual and systemic level. As a philosophy, it can be engaged with by acknowledging personal privileges, confronting acts and systems of racial discrimination, and/or working to change personal racial biases.

BIPOC: an acronym that stands for Black, Indigenous and People of Color

Racism: the belief that groups of humans possess different behavioral traits corresponding to physical appearance and can be divided based on the superiority of one race over another. It may also mean prejudice, discrimination, or antagonism directed against other people because they are of a different ethnicity. Modern variants of racism are often based in social perceptions of biological differences between peoples. These views can take the form of social actions, practices or beliefs, or political systems in which different races are ranked as inherently superior or inferior to each other, based on presumed shared inheritable traits, abilities, or qualities.

Person/People of Color: a term primarily used to describe any person who is not considered "white."

Pluralization of Native Nation Names: the following Journal entries use the same form for Native nation names in both the singular and the plural, as it recognizes the self-identifying name and language of a specific Native nation or group.

Introduction
Cape Cod Camino Way Project

Germination in 2020

The Cape Cod Camino Way is a walking pilgrimage across Cape Cod to increase awareness and deepen understanding about issues of racial and social justice through examining the local history, culture, peoples, and their stories. Originating as a personal pilgrimage across Cape Cod in the summer of 2020, I've documented that journey here to share my experience and learning, and provide you the resources and support to consider a similar project of your own. In the following pages, you will come to understand Cape Cod as you never experienced it before. You will learn about some of the people who came before you, hear their stories and perspectives, and connect this knowledge to current social justice issues (economy, health care, education, environment, policing, religion, the arts, cultural organizations, etc.). My hope is that through reading about this summer walking experience I created for myself and others, you will be exposed to new ideas, facts, beliefs, and stories that will touch you deeply and challenge you to investigate further. The Cape Cod Camino Way is a pathway of both individual and collective discovery and healing. There is also fun to be had along the way in exploring out-of-the-way places and overlooked gems of history and culture hidden right in front of you.

This journal is laid out as both a reflection on my 2020 walks across Cape Cod, and as an invitation to explore one or more of the walks on your own, with your family, or in a small group. You may even be tempted to try all 8 walks, allowing you to touch on every town on Cape Cod and provide you with the full experience of the Cape Cod Camino Way.

Some Context for this Pilgrimage

As a 60-year-old woman of Irish and Polish descent, I grew up visiting Cape Cod every summer for a precious, week-long vacation with my family. I later lived on the Cape for three summers during college, then became permanently attached to the peninsula when I bought my first home here in 1999. Since 2013, I have lived in Brewster full-time, only crossing the bridge to the "mainland" occasionally for consulting and higher education work. Through my involvement in higher education, I became exposed to theories, approaches, and perspectives such as multiculturalism, diversity, equity, and inclusion. I worked as an "ally" for decades to create and sustain programs and services that meet the needs of all students. Starting with my Master's degree program at UMass Amherst in the early 1980s, and continuing throughout my career, I sought to understand the systems I was a part of, and to change them for the better. What I had been doing, however, was woefully inadequate, and I made a lot of mistakes along the way.

The winter and spring of 2020 saw numerous Black men and women killed at the hands of police. Our country was struggling through the most divisive political dynamic since the Civil War. The Covid-19 pandemic began to creep into our lives, infecting thousands, then millions, and changing every aspect of our existence (travel, work, family relationships, technology, education, the economy, health care...the list goes on). Here on Cape Cod, the historical, political, and social context mirrored that of the country: divisiveness; complacency and complicity in perpetuating a system of economic and racial injustice; an aging population with a strained health care system; and a sense of isolation from the "mainland." I heard more than one neighbor implore: "Can't we just close the bridges?" (Yes, Cape Cod is technically a peninsula with a canal that cuts if off from the mainland of Massachusetts.) I knew that meant not just to visitors and Covid, but to the issues of social and racial justice happening "over there."

I became more agitated, more curious about what was happening all around me. Out of this period of incubation, confusion, and chaos, the kernel of an idea was born: instead of travelling to another country to experience their culture, history, and social condition, I could walk the full peninsula of Cape Cod—all 15 towns—and learn about the local peoples and their stories, especially those largely unknown to me. Due to Covid, I couldn't make my usual international summer travel experience, but I could explore other cultures, histories, and peoples right in my own backyard. So I decided to undertake a walking pilgrimage through every town on Cape Cod to better understand issues of racial and social justice locally.

Pilgrimage and the Original Camino Way

As a seeker of knowledge and understanding in areas as diverse as history, spirituality, Eastern philosophy, wellness, nature, sports, politics, and social justice issues, I consider myself a perpetual learner. I also know that emotional, physical, and spiritual "intelligences" are real and inform my approach to understanding the world around me—e.g. What do I know? How do I know this? Where did this understanding come from? What influenced me? What do I *not* know? Where can I seek a wider understanding of a topic, an opinion, or a belief different than the one I hold? How can I share this experience and knowledge I've gained with others?

All of these questions spun in my head after the killing of George Floyd on May 25, 2020, and I began to conceptualize the series of walks that I eventually titled the Cape Cod Camino Way. Walking has long been seen as the best way to get out of your head. "Friedrich Nietzsche, a life-long walker, remarked: "Never trust a thought that didn't come by walking." I concur with Nietzsche's mindset, and add that the practice of walking mindfully is to discover the overlapping points between history and everyday life, the way to find the essence in people and places of interest, both natural and cultural.

Let's explore the word "pilgrimage" a bit more to understand why, in 2020, I titled this project a "Camino Way." As **Phil Cousineau** explains in his 1998 book ***The Art of Pilgrimage: The Seeker's Guide to Making Travel Sacred***:

> "...pilgrimage is a **transformative journey to a sacred center**...a journey of risk and renewal.... a powerful metaphor for any journey with the purpose of finding something that matters deeply to the traveler...Pilgrimage is the kind of journeying that marks just this move from mindless to mindful, soulless to soulful travel...by definition it is life-changing."

He continues later:
> "Pilgrim has its roots in the Latin per agrum, **"through the field."** This ancient image suggests a curious soul who walks beyond known boundaries, crosses fields, touching the earth with a destination in mind and a purpose in heart."

The year 2020 marked the 400th anniversary of the Pilgrims' arrival in Provincetown before they settled in Plymouth. Provincetown 400, a variety of exhibits, events, and opportunities for learning organized by the Pilgrim Monument and Provincetown Museum, was postponed due to Covid. I planned on following the journey of the Pilgrims and connecting it to the experiences of the Nauset and Wampanoag peoples, both of those the Pilgrims first met and of those who currently live here on Cape Cod. I knew some of the familiar narrative of the first meeting of the Pilgrims and Wampanoag, but I also knew I needed to learn the accurate story. As you will see in walk descriptions of later Journal entries, it turned out that the Pilgrims and their story haunted me throughout the summer and into fall of 2020.

So, What Is The Camino Way?

An anglicized term for the *Camino de Santiago*, or "Way of St. James," it is **a network of pilgrimages of Medieval Origin that lead to the Cathedral of Santiago de Compostela in Galicia,** an autonomous community in the northwest of Spain. Legend has it that the remains of the Apostle, Saint James the Great, were buried there. The city is, in fact, named after the apostle: Santiago de Compostela roughly translates to "Saint James of the field of the star."

The Camino de Santiago has been listed as a UNESCO World Heritage site for its centuries-old role in encouraging cultural exchange between peoples from all over Europe and the world. More than just a pilgrimage today, **the Camino de Santiago is a unique experience that attracts hundreds of thousands of people walking to find themselves, find their God, and find each other**. I considered my walks across Cape Cod a "Camino Way," a pilgrimage. Hence, the Cape Cod Camino Way.

Cape Cod Times **Letter to the Editor**
May 31, 2020

Over the past few weeks, we have seen the continuation of decades of racial profiling and violence against Black and brown people. George Floyd was murdered this week in MN by officers sworn to protect him as well as every other community member. Ahmaud Arbery was targeted and murdered in Georgia by a father and son, and filmed by a third person now charged in his death. Christian Cooper was just trying to watch birds in Central Park and became the target of a white woman "in fear of her life" because he started filming her and her dog. In her apology she said she is not racist and meant no harm to "that man". Br[e]onna Taylor was shot 20 times in her own home by police who never identified themselves when they entered. What do all of these incidents have to do with a group of white women on Cape Cod? With all of us who live on Cape Cod?

We are all connected in the human condition. We are all part of this imperfect democracy, formed from a rebellion against repression and violence, but one that never removed the vestiges of the institution of slavery through true reconciliation and empowerment. We are responsible for the continued violence and deaths of our brothers and sisters of color.

Over the past six months several white women from various backgrounds came together to continue to examine our privilege and prejudices that were ingrained in us through our culture- education, churches families, laws and policies. Together we read the book White Fragility by Robin DiAngelo and spent Sunday afternoons exploring the concepts of white privilege and what is our responsibility NOW. This week's collective examples of systemic racism, many exposed through video, require us to speak out. It is painful to watch Black and brown people systematically profiled, violently murdered and discriminated against in repeated fashion. For those of us in mixed race families and friendship groups, it is hard to watch our loved ones in fear. It makes us angry to live in a country that has changed so little in our lifetimes as we continue to witness the injustices we saw this week, we see every week.

The current system reproduces racial harm, inequal treatment, and outright violence. It takes honesty and courage to look within oneself and see what a lifetime of privilege looks like. It takes commitment to call out our public leaders, police forces, the medical establishment and economic systems that are biased against Black, brown, and poor people. The starkly disproportionate death rate for Americans of color- Black, brown, Native American- during this pandemic is another example of systemic failure to ensure the health and well-being of all our citizens.

What can we do? We can be willing to examine our assumptions, attitudes and beliefs. We can educate ourselves by reading Ta-Nehisi Coates, Michelle Alexander and Robin DiAngelo among others. We can work to get past our defensiveness. We can form coalitions with other white people to explore in our own spaces the difficult questions that need to be asked.

We can ask if our police departments, schools, churches, arts organizations, and other community groups are exploring issues of racial and social justice in hiring and all their programs. We can ensure that anti-racism training happens and is funded appropriately. We can hold these groups accountable.

We can grieve together. We can acknowledge the anger and outrage. We can partner with groups such as the *NAACP, Southern Poverty Law Center and Black Lives Matter. We can promote true dialogue, understanding, and learning. We can be humble. We can be courageous. We can be part of the solution. We have power to speak out, to DO SOMETHING. Please, do it NOW!*

Licia Fields
Brewster, MA

Peggy Jablonski
Brewster, MA

Colleen Holden
Centerville, MA

Jennie Mignone
Brewster, MA

My Process

Over the course of the summer of 2020, I conducted research on issues of racial and social justice in each of the towns on Cape Cod and created a walking map. In order to touch all towns on the Cape, as well as remain as safe as possible with challenges like traffic and a lack of sidewalks, I mapped out 5 of the 8 walks on the bike paths. I decided that there would be a rhythm to each week: plan and research people and places on Monday and Tuesday; on Wednesday walk 10 to 15 miles that connects at least two towns; process the interactions and learning into a Blog for the Facebook site by Thursday evening; share a Facebook Live Video on Friday mornings; and lastly, hold a coffee hour conversation on Saturdays at a local coffee shop.

We would examine such questions as:

What did we learn this week?

What was the story we listened to, and how does it impact me?

What am I going to do now?

What do I still need to learn more about?

The Process Continues:
Join the Cape Cod Camino Way Facebook Group
www.facebook.com/groups/capecodcaminoway/

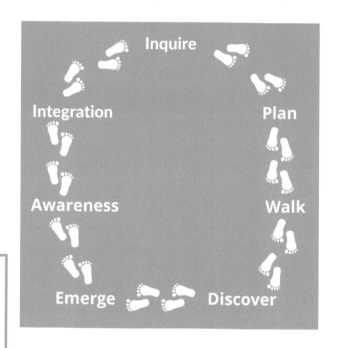

Each week, approximately 200 people interacted with the Camino Way website by viewing the pictures, reading the blog, and watching the video. Due to Covid restrictions, after two weeks the coffee hour aspect of the project was replaced with the Facebook Live Video.

A total of 43 individuals joined me on the walks, with six people joining multiple walks, and one friend participating in all eight. We would gather early, before the heat of the day, and start with a blessing for our time together and our walk over Native American land. I provided an overview for the day ahead, including major sites we would see and the issues we would talk about along the way. Each week had one or more themes related to the places and peoples we interacted with or the cycle of the calendar (e.g. looking at The Declaration of Independence and the Constitution around July 4th).

I shared both historical and current information with the participants, offering them an understanding of their local area of which they were mostly unaware. I tried to create the opportunity for deep learning and dialogue among the participants and with people from various backgrounds and organizations we met along the way.

Over the course of the summer, I was interviewed by the local media, including WCAI (the local NPR radio station), *Cape Cod Times*, *The Provincetown Independent*, and *Barnstable Patriot*. A few participants also wrote about their experiences on Facebook or in local media sources.

Cape Cod Camino Way In the Media:

NEWS

Capewide pilgrimage offers a fuller version of history

Brewster woman hopes to turn what she learned on 8-week walk into action

Ethan Genter egenter@capecodonline.com
Published 5:48 p.m. ET Aug. 26, 2020

View Comments

OP-ED

Walking the Cape Cod Camino

An exercise in reflecting on systemic racism in a privileged community

BY CANDACE PERRY · SEP 3, 2020

Don't just stand there: Do something!

Kathleen Schatzberg
Published 6:49 a.m. ET Jul. 23, 2020

In This Place

"The Cape Cod Camino Way," Walking Cape Cod to Learn About Racism

CAI | By Kathryn Eident

▶ LISTEN · 4:44

In This Place

Lessons Learned from the Cape Cod Camino Way

CAI | By Kathryn Eident

▶ LISTEN · 4:51

Local public radio for the Cape, Coast and Islands
90.1 91.1 94.3
A service of **WGBH**

Map of Cape Cod Camino Way

Walking with a Purpose

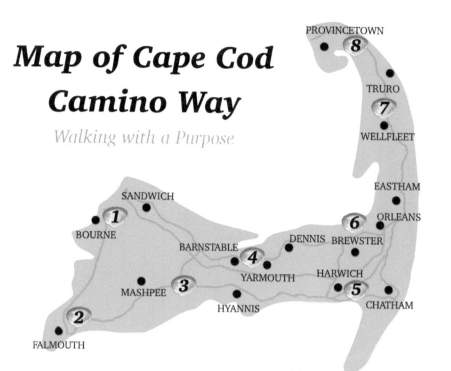

PROVINCETOWN

8

TRURO

7

WELLFLEET

EASTHAM

SANDWICH

1

ORLEANS

6

BOURNE

BREWSTER

DENNIS

BARNSTABLE

4

MASHPEE

3

YARMOUTH

HARWICH

5

HYANNIS

CHATHAM

2

FALMOUTH

WALK 1
The Canal Walks – Step by Step:
A Walk for Social & Racial Justice

WALK 2
From Katharine to Rachel:
Statues of Women and Signs of
Our Times

WALK 3
Black, Indigenous and
People of Color on Cape Cod

WALK 4
Walking the Bay Side:
Economics and Justice Issues

WALK 5
Focus on Health:
Mind/Body/Spirit

WALK 6
Cape Economy and the Institution
of Slavery & The Environment
and the National Seashore

WALK 7
Cultural Kaleidoscope: The Arts

WALK 8
Land's End: Pilgrims, Poets, and
Provincetown

Cape Cod Camino Way

1. The Canal Walks – Step by Step: A Walk for Social & Racial Justice
July 8, 2020
Route: Cape Cod Canal Bikeway (both sides) – 13.5 miles
Towns: Buzzards Bay, Bourne, Sagamore, Sandwich

2. From Katharine to Rachel: Statues of Women and Signs of Our Times
July 15, 2020
Route: Shining Sea Bikeway – 12 miles
Towns: Falmouth, Woods Hole

3. Black, Indigenous and People of Color on Cape Cod: Past and Present Woven Together
July 22, 2020
Route: Mashpee Wampanoag Museum to Zion Union Heritage Museum – 14 miles
Towns: Mashpee, Cotuit, Centerville, Osterville, Marstons Mills, Barnstable, Hyannis

4. Walking the Bay Side: Economic and Justice Issues
July 29, 2020
Route: Cape Cod Community College to Cape Cod Center for the Arts – 11 miles
Towns: Barnstable, Yarmouth Port, Dennis

5. Focus on Health: Mind/Body/Spirit
August 5, 2020
Route: Cape Cod Rail Trail to Atwood House Museum – 14 miles
Towns: Harwich, Chatham

6. Cape Economy and the Institution of Slavery & The Environment and the National Seashore
August 12, 2020
Route: Brewster Snowy Owl to Cape Cod National Seashore Salt Pond Visitor Center – 11 miles
Towns: Brewster, Orleans, Eastham

7. Cultural Kaleidoscope: The Arts
August 19, 2020
Route: Lecount Hollow Beach to Pamet River Trails – 11.5 miles
Towns: Wellfleet, Truro

8. Land's End: Pilgrims, Poets, and Provincetown
August 26, 2020
Route: Truro Public Library to Provincetown Town Center – 12 miles
Towns: Truro, Provincetown

Walk 1
The Canal Walks – Step by Step:
A Walk for Social & Racial Justice

"Walking is the best way to get out of your head."

-Phil Cousineau, *The Art of Pilgrimage: The Seeker's Guide to Making Travel Sacred*

July 8, 2020

Towns: Buzzards Bay, Bourne, Sagamore, Sandwich

Route: Cape Cod Canal Bikeway, both sides

Morning Walk: North side of the Canal, from Sandwich Recreation Area (Freezer Rd off 6A) to the Tidal Flats Recreation Area (Bell Rd) – 6. 5 miles

Afternoon Walk: South side of the Canal, from Buzzards Bay Park (Canal St) to Scusset Beach State Reservation – 7 miles

Total: 13.5 miles

Site:

• Cape Cod Canal

Issues Explored:

• Overview of the project and themes – What is a "Camino Way?"
• Connection to the Fourth of July and the founding documents of our country- The Declaration of Independence and the Constitution
• Life for Black, Indigenous and People of Color (BIPOC) in the United States, and on Cape Cod

Morning Walk

Watching the rushing water flowing through the Cape Cod Canal, I felt the current pulling me downstream to see what was around the bend. The Canal unfolded slowly to reveal its true nature. I believed that would be true of exploring Cape Cod by foot, one step at a time.

To be on a pilgrimage is to go on both an inner and outer journey. So began my journey of Cape Cod during the summer of 2020. I chose to use the time during the Covid-19 pandemic to explore racial and social injustice right here on the Cape, as well as undertake my own work to deepen my awareness of my privilege and the connected responsibility to both make and support change.

I stood close to the opening of the Cape Cod Canal, near the Sandwich Marina, with three other women, and thought about the weeks ahead: I would be walking to touch each town on the Cape with an open heart and inquiring mind, to see beneath the surface of our beautiful, tranquil peninsula and understand more fully what life is like for people of color. My sister Marie was there with me, and I was grateful for her support that day and all days. She provided important logistical and moral support during this and two other walks over the summer.

I wore a purple T-shirt with a silhouette of the Cape and a quahog shell on it—**purple and white, and a symbol of the Wampanoag, the Native American people of this region.** I chose the clam shell as a symbol of the Cape Cod Camino Way, modeled after the scallop shell that symbolizes the original Camino Way walking pilgrimage in Spain. According to the Wampanoag people, the shell has the quality of holding record of the journey, and of an entire life span. For me, the Camino Way logo represents life, liberty, and justice for all.

I started the day with a **blessing on the Native American Lands,** and on my Camino Way:

The People of the First Light, the Wampanoag, honor the earth and creator. Bless this journey across Cape Cod as we travel on the lands of native peoples. May I honor those who have passed this way before me. May I be open to listening and reflecting through a process of inner and outer exploration. May I be changed, my commitment to eradicating social injustice strengthened, and my work around anti-racism informed for the future.

I shared with my small, but hearty group of three others what we would experience today and the topics we would explore. We would examine quotes from founding documents—The Declaration of Independence and the Constitution— to ask important questions about life, liberty, and the pursuit of happiness, such as:

- What rights exist for all peoples? What rights are denied to some?

- Did Black, Indigenous and People of Color give their consent to be governed when their lands were taken from them or when they were brought here through the institution of slavery?

- "All men are created equal." If the use of the term "men" in 1776 included all people, that would mean women, those enslaved, and the indigenous peoples here before European colonization would be covered by that term. So why does "men" sometimes mean all people, but in the case of our founding documents, only mean white, privileged, land-owning men?

- The Declaration of Independence declares that people have the right to abolish the government when it becomes destructive to the preservation of their rights. Isn't that what the 2020 protests for social and racial justice across the country, as well as the world, were essentially demanding?

I started on our morning walk from Sandwich to Bourne with a determination to delve deeply into this place I call home, as well as this country I love dearly. I wanted to be open to whatever emerged along the way, and I took in some deep breaths to center and ground me, to heighten my awareness that I was undertaking a sacred pilgrimage as well as an outdoor walk with friends. At a rest stop, I read part of **Nikole Hannah-Jones' essay, "The Idea of America" from "The 1619 Project" of *The New York Times Magazine*:**

*"**The United States is a nation founded on both an ideal and a lie.** Our Declaration of Independence, approved on July 4, 1776, proclaims that "all men are created equal" and "endowed by their Creator with certain unalienable rights." But the white men who drafted those words did not believe them to be true for the hundreds of thousands of black people in their midst. **"Life, Liberty and the pursuit of Happiness" did not apply to fully one-fifth of the country."***

I also noted that **Native Americans were thus described in our Declaration of Independence:**

*"[King George] has excited domestic insurrections amongst us, and has endeavoured to bring on the inhabitants of our frontiers, the **merciless Indian Savages**, whose known rule of warfare, is an undistinguished destruction of all ages, sexes and conditions."*

The American practice of enslaving Africans started in Virginia, 157 years before our Declaration of Independence. It was ingrained into the foundation of American colonies, with the labor of Black and Brown people providing the "machinery" to fuel the fortunes of white America, and continues to this day. It took a violent civil war to end the institution of slavery, but immediately after that, practices were instituted to maintain white supremacy in all areas. I shared with my fellow walkers that, as of today, we have not truly reckoned with this legacy that continues to infuse every aspect of our lives: our economy, health care, housing, employment, education, government, and so on.

We walked into a headwind that morning, stopping to watch the herons catch fish and sharing our stories related to democracy. I thought about how **Black and Indigenous people are always walking into a headwind, being judged through unconscious bias and discriminatory practices inherent in our systems.** As we were sharing our personal stories of life in the pandemic, I heard the church bells toll nearby and asked for us to pause and be mindful of the sounds around us. I was reminded that walking the Canal on a beautiful day in the middle of the week was a privilege that many people don't have due to the demands of work and family.

> Stopping and paying honor to nature, to music, or to just take a pause to refocus became a part of every walk over the course of the summer.

At one point in the conversation, near the **Aptucxet Trading Post**, we talked about the protests going on around the country over police killings of black and brown people and their root in systemic racism. We spoke of being terrified to see what happened in Washington, D.C.—a president clearing the plaza in front of a church through violent means for a photo op with a Bible. I shared with my friends how watching that night unfold on television had a profound impact on me. I went down to the beach and created a video of me reciting the **Preamble to the Constitution**, adding that we are an **imperfect constitutional democracy**, not a dictatorship. I posted it on Facebook to take a stand. I'm sure I had more than one person "unfriend" me.

We finished our morning walk at the Tidal Flats Recreation Area in Bourne. I asked Lauren and Amy, who would be leaving me at this point, what they were taking away from their morning walk?

"Seeing the natural beauty of the Cape was another bonus! As a Gardener by profession, I'm grateful my work brings me outside most of the year. I think that's another reason I resonated with the Native American influence on our walks. Also, I had never walked the the Cape Cod Canal, where a blue heron seemed to follow us, and walked the bike path and beaches in Falmouth and Woods Hole for the first time.

I look forward to more walks in the future, continuing to understand the issues of social justice right in my own backyard, and committing to making a difference right where I live. "

-Lauren Miklavic

Lauren Miklavic, a creative landscape artist and designer from the Cape, would end up walking all eight weeks with me over the summer. She only missed the south side of the Canal, and returned to complete the full journey of the Camino Way.

Afternoon Walk

After a warm morning of walking, I crossed the Bourne Bridge (in a car!), and found myself above the Canal looking out to Buzzards Bay and wondering about the lived experiences of all people who call Cape Cod home. What stories would I discover on my future walks? Who did I need to listen to, open my heart to?

We gathered at a picnic table at the Buzzards Bay Recreation Area, next to Massachusetts Maritime Academy. My sister, Marie, and my dear friend of several decades, Linda, joined me for a few snacks to set the stage for our 6.5-mile afternoon walk. We viewed the NPR video of **Frederick Douglass' descendants delivering his July 5, 1852 address, "What to the Slave Is the Fourth of July?"** and reflected on Douglass' truths:

"I am not included within the pale of glorious anniversary! Your high independence only reveals the immeasurable distance between us. The blessings in which you, this day, rejoice, are not enjoyed in common. The rich inheritance of justice, liberty, prosperity and independence, bequeathed by your fathers, is shared by you, not by me. The sunlight that brought light and healing to you, has brought stripes and death to me. This Fourth of July is yours, not mine. You may rejoice, I must mourn..."

Portrait of Frederick Douglass, National Portrait Gallery, Smithsonian Institution

The powerful and passionate voices of the the teenage great-grandchildren of Douglass who recited these words resounded deeply within me. We continued our walk on the south side of the Canal, talking about what the Fourth of July meant in our families and how divided our country is right now. For Marie and me, July 4th has always been a difficult holiday, as our brother Paul was killed in a car accident on this day in 1978, when he was just 16 years old. Although he's been gone for over 40 years, his spirit remains vivid in our lives, and I felt his presence with us as we walked the Canal.

Linda and I share a history of thirty years as colleagues in higher education. We worked with educators across the country and here in New England to facilitate change in our institutions towards more equity and inclusiveness, and by extension, have changed ourselves. We spoke of our roles in our careers as mentors and sponsors of others, people of color and white, and rededicated ourselves to do even more now. We spoke of recent trips we took together to Ireland and Cuba, to explore Celtic spirituality and Cuban culture.

At the mid-point of our walk, we stopped for a juice break and honored the founding of our country by reading excerpts of the Constitution of the United States. We acknowledged that **the Northern States compromised by enshrining the practice of enslaving people in the Constitution,** with the capture and transportation of Africans to the United States continuing until 1808, and the institution itself existing until the end of the Civil War.

> *"Representatives and direct Taxes shall be apportioned among the several States which may be included within this Union, according to their respective Numbers, which shall be determined by adding to the whole Number of free Persons, **including those bound to Service for a Term of Years, and excluding Indians not taxed, three fifths of all other Persons."***
> *-Constitution of the United States of America: Article I, Section 2*

We reached the end of the Canal at Scusset Beach Recreation Area and celebrated our accomplishment of the 13.5-mile walk with a yoga pose—**Warrior II.** I've taken a photo of Warrior poses on many of my travels, and **the strength, grounding, and sense of rising up from the core of one's being perfectly symbolized our first walk that day.**

Reflections from Walkers

Amy: "I never walked the Canal before and the opportunity to reflect on these issues while walking is a gift."

Marie: "A large container ship passed us in the Canal, almost filling the waterway with the fruits of our economy. How far we have come from 1620! Or have we?"

"I enthusiastically joined Peggy and her sister Marie on the second half of the inaugural CC Camino Way Walk on July 8, 2020. It is always inspiring and rejuvenating to walk the Canal, especially so on a beautiful summer day, though in the midst of a worldwide pandemic and racial, economic, and social unrest and upheaval across our Country. Yet another example of the privilege we have.

During this summer of pandemic, continued racial injustice, social activism toward truly making Black Lives Matter, and the rise of visible and vocal white nationalism in our country, Peggy developed an action plan to listen, learn and act while walking the byways of Cape Cod. We had several talks regarding this concept and how to focus it on listening, learning more deeply about the history and origins of 400 years of racism in America and early instances of it on Cape Cod. Also to focus on the ways the varying degrees of privilege, or lack thereof, affect everything we and others experience."
-Linda Ragosta, Kingston, MA

• Research the walk location, sites along the way, and any supporting documents or stories you'd like to share with your group. **Always have more material than you have time to share.**

• Be open to stopping for rest breaks, as **others may need to refuel mind/body/spirit in a different way than you.**

• Walking alone is a good way to experience the world around you; walking with others brings you connection and conversation to expand or change your experience. Both are valuable.

• Our country's founding documents, **The Declaration of Independence and the Constitution, are inherently racist, classist, sexist, and anti-Native American.** Be a critical consumer of information.

• Expose yourself to alternative sources, not alternative facts. **Listen to podcasts and readings by Black, Indigenous and other People of Color about familiar material, like the country's founding documents, to examine taught narratives from new perspectives.** Listen to the hit musical *Hamilton*, Frederick Douglass' address on the Fourth of July, and his great-grandchildren's modern version.

• Take LOTS of water – there are no places to purchase food or drinks on either side of the Canal, except near the beginning or end of each route.

• There are no public restrooms along the bike path. Be open-minded and prepared to visit the "outdoor restrooms." Enough said.

• Take meaningful photos so you can reflect on your trip later, then post them to your social media with commentary and questions to explore with your broader community.

• Enjoy the beauty of the Cape Cod Canal, the history alongside it, and the majesty of the Bourne and Sagamore Bridges. Thirteen miles is doable, but you will be tired at the end. Get takeout for dinner!

Resources:
Aptucxet Trading Post and Museums at Aptucxet
https://www.bournehistoricalsociety.org/aptucxet-museum/
"The Idea of America" by Nikole Hannah-Jones from *The New York Times Magazine*'s "The 1619 Project"
www.pulitzercenter.org/1619
"What to the Slave Is the Fourth of July?" by Frederick Douglass' from his July 5, 1852 address and delivered by his descendants from NPR
https://www.youtube.com/watch?v=NBe5qbnkqoM

Create Your Own Walk with Friends and Family

Cape Cod Canal Bikeway: Walk, Bike, Rollerblade or Skateboard

Be prepared with snacks and plenty of water as there are limited sources at either end of the bike path for refilling water bottles or purchasing supplies. Plan at least three hours per side of the Canal if walking, in order to enjoy some breaks and a few side detours.

Consider dropping a car at each end of the Canal and walking from one car to another to provide transportation. If biking, bike up and back the same side for a 13 to 14-mile ride.

Use the resources provided in this chapter on the founding documents of the United States, and critiques of them, to discuss with your group along the way. Stop and use one of the quotes to engender discussion. Encourage all members of the group to speak, without judgement or argument from anyone. Encourage people of all ages to tell their stories. Remain open to what you may hear and learn from each other.

Option 1: North Side from Buzzards Bay to Sagamore – 6.5 miles

Start at the Buzzards Bay Recreation Area, next to Massachusetts Maritime Academy. Admire the T.S. Kennedy ship at dock, the iconic Railroad Bridge, and the Bourne Bridge in the distance. Pass the Bourne Scenic Park and climb the hill to the Bournedale Hills interpretive trail in the woods for a little relief from the sun and wind. Look for herring in the Herring Run (April – June) and stop at the Visitor Center. Continue under the Sagamore Bridge and walk the side paths of the Sagamore Hill Loop trail for impressive views. End at Scusset Beach State Reservation, with its fishing and gathering areas, and a wide, sandy beach for swimming.

Option 2: South Side from Sandwich to Bourne – 7 miles

Start at the Cape Cod Canal Region Visitors Center and, if open, take in the exhibits. If not, read the interpretive signs outside. Gaze at the opening of the Canal and read about its construction online.

Walk by the Sandwich Marina and admire the homes along both sides of the Canal. Cross under the Sagamore Bridge, following the winding Canal toward the Bourne Bridge. Visit the Aptucxet Trading Post and the Museums at Aptucxet, a 12-acre campus consisting of a replica of the Pilgrim Trading Post built by the Plymouth colonists in 1628 to trade with the local Wampanoag people and Dutch traders. Also look for the Gray Gables Railroad Station, built to serve President Grover Cleveland, and the Joseph Jefferson Windmill, now serving as an art studio and gallery. The site also features a replica of a 19th century saltworks, a coastal schooner, and numerous gardens. Finish this side of the bike path at the Tidal Flats Recreation Area by looking out to the other end of the Canal in Buzzards Bay.

Walk 2
From Katharine to Rachel – Statues of Women and Signs of Our Times

> *"The botany I was taught was reductionist, mechanistic, and strictly objective. Plants were reduced to objects; they were not subjects. The way botany was conceived and taught didn't seem to leave much room for a person who thought the way I did...My natural inclination was to see relationships, to seek the threads that connect the world, to join instead of divide...To walk the science path I had stepped off the path of indigenous knowledge."*
>
> -Robin Wall Kimmerer, *Braiding Sweetgrass: Indigenous Wisdom, Scientific Knowledge and the Teachings of Plants*

July 16, 2020

Towns: Falmouth, Woods Hole

Route: Shining Sea Bikeway from County Rd, North Falmouth to Woods Hole Oceanographic Institute – 12 miles

Sites:
- Sippewissett Marsh
- Falmouth Town Green
- Katharine Lee Bates statue
- Woods Hole Oceanographic Institution (WHOI)
- Rachel Carson statue
- Northeast Fisheries Science Center of the National Oceanic and Atmospheric Administration (NOAA)

Issues Explored:
- Women and People of Color in Science
- Katharine Lee Bates and "America the Beautiful"

While preparing for this walk, I began to realize that creating the Cape Cod Camino Way was similar to producing a mini-series of eight shows, each requiring their own preparation, content, background research, route planning, logistics, engaging company, good weather, and stamina. Thankfully, I had all of these for Walk 2. Each week I prepared an itinerary for the walk with quotes from relevant writings, songs, poems, or interviews I had conducted in advance. I sought to make the walk inspirational for anyone joining me and for those following via the blog and Cape Cod Camino Way Facebook page (which is still active and available to join!).

Given the number of science and research-related institutions in Woods Hole (the Woods Hole Oceanographic Institute or WHOI, the Northeast Fisheries Science Center of the National Oceanographic and Atmospheric Administration or NOAA, and several others), I decided to focus on **the places where women and people of color have been excluded from science as well as where they have made significant contributions.** Having worked in higher education for over 30 years, including at both Massachusetts Institute of Technology and Worcester Polytechnic Institute, I am aware of significant impediments to the advancement of women and people of color in the science fields. **These impediments are rooted in systemic racism and sexism in education at all levels, including a lack of mentoring towards advanced degrees**. We explored these issues with women scientists, high school students, and parents over the course of our five-hour walk through these two towns. We also stopped at two statues dedicated to women, which raised the question: how many statues of women exist on Cape Cod, and for what purpose? I hoped to find additional markers of significant contributions by women and people of color over the summer as we trekked Cape Cod.

At the beginning of the Shining Sea Bikeway in North Falmouth, I discovered I'd left my notes for the event, with all the quotes and songs I wanted to share and reference...on my kitchen table. Even though I had planned and prepared for the walk, I then had to improvise with what I could remember, and pull up what I could on my phone when I happened to have a signal (which is often in question on the Cape). I took a deep breath to settle my disappointment and stepped off with Lauren to start the day. We shared our intentions for the walk, paying tribute to the Native lands we would travel and asking for safe passage.

About 2 miles on the path, I rolled onto my right ankle, fell onto my hip, and sustained road rash on my leg. Shaken up a bit, I took a sip of water and gathered my thoughts to regroup. "Be more aware of your surroundings, let go of your disappointment about forgetting your notes, and everything will be ok" I whispered to myself. If my ankle was throbbing in another mile, I would turn around and get the car. I got up, dusted off, and stepped forward into the peaceful woods and bogs surrounding the path.

For the next few miles, Lauren and I talked about the challenges of being a woman in a non-traditional field such as science. I shared the story of my sister-in-law, **Jillian McLeod, a professor at the Coast Guard Academy and one of the only Black women in the country with a PhD in theoretical math. Her work on equity and inclusion at the CGA is making a difference in the education of thousands of students.** We both relayed times in our careers (me in higher education and Lauren, marketing and, now, landscape design) where we confronted blatant and subtle examples of sexism and harassment. Unfortunately, we both had far too many examples to share.

For a diversion, we discussed one of our favorite places to travel: Ireland! I told her stories from my ten trips to Ireland, including golfing over 50 times on the Emerald Isle. We were transported to the west coast of Ireland by the similar views of bogs and inlets of the Sippewissett Marsh we were walking through. Due to the Covid pandemic, we both had travel plans cancelled in 2020. When would we be able to travel internationally again, and once possible, where would we like to go now? Have our plans changed because of Covid? Has it made some places more or less desirable or compelling?

We also discussed good books, and I shared a current favorite: *Braiding Sweetgrass* by Robin Wall Kimmerer. **Trained traditionally as a botanist, Kimmerer brings the lenses of her Native Potawatomi background and ecological consciousness to her understanding of the earth and her plants.** She weaves her science background together with deep wisdom from indigenous knowledge. For both enlightening and engaging reading, treat yourself and others to a copy of *Braiding Sweetgrass*.

Prior to the walk, I enjoyed a conversation with **Claudia Womble, who is working with the National Oceanic and Atmospheric Administration (NOAA) and the 5 other major institutions in Woods Hole to implement the recommendations from Robert Livingston's 2018 *Woods Hole Diversity and Inclusion Report and Recommendations*.** Issues such as the lack of diversity in numbers and programming, absence of cultural competence among the staff, and the presence of apathy, skepticism, micro-aggressions, and overt racism in the work culture were all present in the findings of the report. The Woods Hole Diversity Initiative outlines plans for recruitment, retention, and accountability around all aspects of diversity and inclusion. This could consist of widening the networks for recruiting faculty and staff, including the diversity of disciplines and types of institutions, such as Historically Black Colleges and Universities, from which to recruit talent to

Woods Hole. Claudia acknowledged that there is much work to be done, just as there is across educational, social, economic, political, environmental, and numerous other landscapes, to include the perspectives of women and people of color.

In front of the Falmouth Library at 11 A.M., **Dana Mock-Muñoz de Luna, from the Marine Biological Lab and the Diversity Initiative, met with us for a conversation about women in science.** We were joined by Patricia Pinto da Silva from NOAA and Lilli Feronti, a 14-year-old Falmouth activist, along with her sister and mother, to discuss and better understand the challenges facing women in science. Why is it important to have various backgrounds and perspectives represented in our research organizations?

Studies show that diverse perspectives strengthen organizations and the work they do in a variety of ways, from the quality of decision-making to the types of questions investigated in research projects. The video of Dana speaking with us is available at the Cape Cod Camino Way Project Facebook page. In front of the Falmouth Library stands the **statue of Katharine Lee Bates, the writer of the song "America the Beautiful."** Not many statues of women exist on Cape Cod, and I wanted to find out more about her and another famous woman, Rachel Carson, whose statue would be at the end of our walk in Woods Hole. Hence the name of this chapter.

Our group of six listened to **the original version of the song, first written as a poem in 1893 when Bates, a professor at Wellesley College, travelled from her hometown of Falmouth across the country and was taken by the scenery.** Bates' original poem extolls the pilgrim's march for freedom across America, with the stanza:

"O great for pilgrim feet
Whose stern, impassioned stress
A thoroughfare for freedom beat
Across the wilderness!
America! America!
God shed His grace on thee
Till paths be wrought through wilds of thought
By pilgrim foot and knee!"

I shared with the group that this verse struck me as odd, and left me questioning. Given that George Floyd was just killed in a brutal fashion, pinned down under a police officer's knee, this led me to ask what "By pilgrim foot and knee" meant? Did it mean that the "white" settlers would take America by knee if necessary?

I remembered reading *Bury My Heart at Wounded Knee* in 8th grade and being very affected by the violence inflicted upon the Native American tribes across the country. My sister, Marie, later explained to me that from her perspective as a long-time choir member, the "knee" phrase was a reference to kneeling in prayer. I still could not erase the image from my mind of Officer Chauvin's face while he kneeled on George Floyd.

The final stanza of the original poem concludes:

"America! America!
God shed His grace on thee
Till nobler men keep once again
Thy whiter jubilee!"

What does this mean? Why was that removed from the next two versions of the song when it was published? Why had I never heard that before? I immediately thought of the current increase in white supremacy-related violence, such as that at the University of Virginia in Charlottesville, or the Mother Emmanuel murders in Charleston, South Carolina. **Restoring America to a "whiter jubilee" was exactly what many of the white supremacy groups were espousing, and the Republican party and then-President were providing support and cover for such actions.**

I knew I had to continue to explore this further, but could not find any insight into its meaning when I looked later. I did discover, however, **a revised version called "America" that the Broadway cast of *Hamilton* performed at a benefit for Broadway Cares/Equity Fights AIDS, and that interweaves the words of Langston Hughes, Bob Marley, and Lin-Manuel Miranda alongside Bates'.** Here are a few verses from this modernized version:

"Let America be America again.
Let it be the dream it used to be...

Oh, let my Land be a Land where liberty is crowned with no false
patriotic grief.
But opportunity is real and life is free.
Equality is in the air we breathe...

There's never been equality for me,
Nor freedom in this homeland of the free...

America, America
God shed His grace on thee.
Who lives, who dies, who tells your story?"

Walking along the shore from Falmouth to Woods Hole with Lilli, her sister, her mom, and the others provided a change of scenery and inspiration. The young people with us were full of hope, energy, and optimism for the future. We talked of opportunities for girls in college and in careers of a variety of fields. **These conversations with thoughtful young people working for change, becoming more aware of social and racial justice issues early in their lives, was the highlight of my day.**

As we arrived at Woods Hole, a doe came onto the path to greet us, and everyone froze in silence. **In this time of Covid, the natural world was alive and filled with surprises.**

We completed the walk in Woods Hole with a photo in front of the **Rachel Carson** statue. **Carson was an American marine biologist who advanced the global environmental movemen**t and influenced the creation of the Environmental Protection Agency, which was currently under assault by the Trump administration. We then celebrated our time together with a nourishing lunch, and shared a sense of gratitude about our day together. Even without my map and notes, the day emerged exactly as it should have!

"I really appreciated the opportunity to slow down and walk from the Kathy Lee Bates statue in the center of Falmouth to the Rachel Carson statue on the Woods Hole waterfront. As we walked we talked about women in science, difference vs diversity, climate change and more - all the while seeing familiar things in new ways and making new friends."

-Patricia Pinto da Silva, Falmouth

Resources:

"America" performed by the Broadway cast of *Hamilton*
https://www.youtube.com/watch?v=rDv-MBqmMak
"America the Beautiful" original lyrics
https://en.wikipedia.org/wiki/America_the_Beautiful
Braiding Sweetgrass: Indigenous Wisdom, Scientific Knowledge and the Teachings of Plants by Robin Wall Kimmerer
https://milkweed.org/book/braiding-sweetgrass
Bury My Heart at Wounded Knee: An Indian History of the American West (1970) by Dee Brown
https://www.amazon.com/Bury-My-Heart-Wounded-Knee/dp/0805086846
"National Institutes of Health addresses the science of diversity" by Hannah A. Valantine and Francis S. Collins
Proceedings of the National Academy of Sciences, Oct. 2015
https://www.pnas.org/content/112/40/12240
"Walking Cape Cod to Learn About Racism" radio interview. WCAI (Cape and Islands NPR station) by Kathryn Eident.
Published July 8, 2020
https://www.capeandislands.org/in-this-place/2020-07-08/the-cape-cod-camino-way-walking-cape-cod-to-learn-about-racism
"Woods Hole Diversity and Inclusion Report and Recommendations" by Robert Livingston on behalf of the Woods Hole Diversity Initiative (2018)

Create Your Own Walk with Friends and Family

Falmouth to Woods Hole: Shining Sea Bikeway Path, Falmouth Town Green, Woods Hole Oceanographic Institute (WHOI)

Option 1: Park in Falmouth Center, meet at the Katharine Lee Bates Statue on the Town Green, walk Main St and turn right on Shore St, then left on Surf Dr walking along the water until it connects with the Shining Sea Bikeway again. Return to the Falmouth Town Green.

Option 2: For a longer walk, drop one car in Falmouth Center and another in Woods Hole. Follow the directions above from Falmouth Center and continue on the Shining Sea Bikeway to Woods Hole, following Woods Hole Rd to the harbor and the Rachel Carson Statue.

Bring plenty of water and snacks to share at the end of the walk or along the way. Public restrooms can be found in Falmouth Center and Woods Hole.

Use the resources provided in this Chapter to discuss women and people of color in science, and quotes from *Braiding Sweetgrass* to discuss indigenous perspectives on nature and science. Examine Bate's song "America the Beautiful" from a critical lens, both the original version of the poem and the song we sing today. What does the song mean to you? Or furthermore, what does the National Anthem mean to you?

In Woods Hole, address the work of Rachel Carson and the Environmental Protection Agency. Research quotes from historical and contemporary women and people of color in science to share and discuss on your walk. Discuss why it is important to have various perspectives represented in science. Be open to what you may learn about science when considering alternative viewpoints to the traditional sources and methods.

Walk 3

Black, Indigenous and People of Color on Cape Cod – Past and Present Woven Together

> *"In particular, learning about the Wampanoag tribe, the Native Americans of the Cape Cod region, impacted me the most. Their history was woven throughout our journey from tip to tail. Learning that Northeastern tribes were matrilineal societies was wonderful! It was also a little heartbreaking to see how slowly women's rites have evolved in our American history experience."*
>
> -Lauren Miklavic, *Walk 3 Participant*

July 22, 2020

Towns: Mashpee, Cotuit, Centerville, Osterville, Marstons Mills, Barnstable, Hyannis

Route: From Mashpee Community Park and Mashpee Wampanoag Indian Museum follow MA Rt 130 five miles to South County Rd, then two miles to Armstrong-Kelley Park in Osterville, then follow Main St two miles to Craigville Beach Rd, then two miles to Smith St, left on Scudder Rd and North St to Zion Union Heritage Museum. – 14 miles

NOTE: There are NO SIDEWALKS for the first 5 miles of this walk. Please do not follow this route.

Sites:
- Mashpee Wampanoag Indian Museum
- Cotuit Center for the Arts
- Cahoon Museum of American Art
- Zion Union Heritage Museum

Issues Explored:
- The stories of the Wampanoag Tribe: history, culture, current recognition
- Plymouth 400, the Pilgrims, and the Mayflower
- Federal recognition of "Indian Tribes"
- Artists of Black, Indigenous and Cape Verdean heritage at the Zion Union Heritage Museum
- Being Black on Cape Cod
- Protest activity around the country and on Cape Cod

As Marie and Lauren gathered at 8 A.M. to start our journey for the day and set our intentions, **two great blue herons flew overhead, their graceful wings outstretched in the humid air.** Herons have been my talisman for decades—watching them in the frog ponds at Forest Park in Springfield as a child, seeing them in the marshes on Cape Cod, and following them on hikes in North Carolina. I even bought a set of folk artist Janet Resnik's pottery dishes hand-painted with herons that I use daily. So I knew immediately when I saw the herons that this was going to be a very special day.

This walk was the most difficult to map out due to the road system and lack of sidewalks along the way. For about 5 miles, we walked on the busy streets of Routes 130 and 28, in the rain, with no sidewalks. Cars and trucks whizzed by us leaving a trail of mist and road dirt in our eyes and mouths. Lauren and I stopped to consider that our route today was a symbol of what has been experienced by people of color and Native Americans for generations: always facing a headwind, a storm, an uphill climb. We used the analogy to brace ourselves as we made progress over our 14-mile route.

We began the day in the hazy sunshine outside the **Mashpee Wampanoag Museum**, which was closed due to the pandemic, but provided a perfect setting for our day's start: a canoe and wetu (a circular home made from trees) where we learned about the *"People of the First Light."* At the wetu, we saw how the Wampanoag people lived on and from the land, using the bark of elm trees as shingles and stumps as benches. Inside we found the remnants of a fire and a few quahog shells. I chose the **quahog, or clam shell**, to represent the Cape Cod Camino Way as a symbolic parallel to the original Camino Way's use of the **scallop shell** to represent its pilgrimage as well as a marker of the path along the way.

Many people wear a shell to represent their Camino Way journey while travelling the paths, and many buildings along the route in Spain are adorned with scallop shells. **For the Cape Cod Camino Way, I wanted a symbol that represented Native American heritage on Cape Cod and our present-day community.** Because the Wampanoag utilized the quahog for food and as wampum (white and purple beads used for trading and jewelry), and because the shellfish industry is still a large part of Cape culture, it made sense for our pilgrimage across Cape Cod to adopt the quahog shell as our official symbol.

The Wampanoag have occupied the same region in the Northeast for over 12,000 years, and have faced the diminishment of their homelands since the colonization of the United States by Europeans. Today, the Mashpee Wampanoag Tribe has approximately 2,600 citizens enrolled, and are currently seeking action by Congress to continue protection of their lands and designation as a federally recognized tribe. This is in response to a notice received on March 27, 2020, from the federal Bureau of Indian Affairs, per an order from the Trump Administration's Secretary of the Interior, that the Mashpee Wampanoag reservation would be disestablished and the land taken out of trust. Out of respect for this struggle, we acknowledged our walking that day on lands once and always owned by the Wampanoag Tribe, and gave thanks for their continued presence.

A few facts that we considered that morning that I found on the Mashpee Wampanoag Museum website and related articles:

• Before the Pilgrims arrived in 1620, European traders had already carried yellow fever to the Northeast coast resulting in the death of two-thirds of the Wampanoag nation (estimated at 45,000).

• When the Pilgrims landed on Cape Cod, the Wampanoag had settlements across Southeastern Massachusetts, the Cape, Eastern Rhode Island, Martha's Vineyard, and Nantucket. They eventually shared their planting methods with the newcomers and taught them about hunting and fishing.

• In 1655, Harvard opened the Indian College to educate Native American youth and convert them to Christianity.

• Between 1675–1678, over 40% of the Wampanoag population was killed in King Philip's War, an armed conflict between a Native coalition and the New England colonists with their Native allies. Large numbers of the remaining healthy males, as well as some women and children, were sold into slavery by the colonists.

• In 1685, the Plymouth Colony granted tribal leaders a deed of 25 square miles of land, and subsequently appointed guardians to limit the Tribe's independence. Ironically, the King of England sided with the Tribe, and Mashpee was recognized as a self-governing Indian district.

• In the Boston Massacre of 1770, Crispus Attucks, a Wampanoag, was killed. Many Wampanoag later fought on behalf of independence in the American Revolution.

• By the mid-1800s, the Massachusetts legislature had revoked the Wampanoag Tribe's governing authority, and in 1869, made members of the Tribe citizens of the state. Then in 1870, the Massachusetts Legislature conveyed the remaining 3,000–5,000 acres owned by the Tribe to the local government to create the town of Mashpee.

• The Wampanoag cultivated varieties of the "three sisters" (beans, squash, and maize or corn) as the staples of their diet, with fish and game as supplements. Women held socio-political, economic, and spiritual roles in their communities. They established a matrilineal system, in which women-controlled property and hereditary status was passed through the maternal line. Moreover, their society was matrifocal, meaning a married couple lived with the woman's family and women elders approved the selection of chiefs or sachems.

As Marie, Lauren, and I reflected on this history that we had heard little of in the past, we were reminded that "victors tell the story." We didn't know that the "first peoples" of these united states were matrilineal. It would take generations for white women to be able to inherit money or property under the democratic republic that the Europeans established, and generations more for women of color to have the same economic rights. And economic rights are just the tip of an iceberg of inequalities facing women, then and now. So we asked ourselves the following questions and engaged in a spirited dialogue as we started our walk:

1. Where would we, as an American society, be if women held a more equal role in the new republic from the beginning?
2. And if women were true partners in the formation and execution of democracy?
3. Where would we be if we had shared the land with the Wampanoag people instead of taking it by force and coercion?
4. What do we still owe the First Peoples?

Lauren and I walked on in the rain following Rt 130, a main road without sidewalks, and with lots of traffic driving too fast for the conditions. We were splattered with road grime and the mist clouded her glasses. We took a break and stood under the protection of an awning at the **Cotuit Center for the Arts**, thinking about the collections in our art museums on Cape Cod. How much art truly reflects the history and stories of who was here, or is currently here? In "normal" years, the Cotuit Center offers a range of programming and provides music, theater, and visual arts to several communities, including underserved, low-income, and at-risk youth. We hoped the arts venues on the Cape were using the pandemic's forced pause to expand their program offerings (music, plays, exhibits, etc.) to incorporate themes, stories, and voices of Black, Indigenous and People of Color.

Further on the day's journey we passed the **Cahoon Museum of American Art**, and were startled by the bright blue-painted trees out front. Lauren, as a landscape designer and naturalist, identified the danger this poses to the trees: *How can they breathe?* As we had just seen how the Wampanoag had used the trees for their homes, and treated nature with respect, it seemed incongruous to us that someone would paint the trees.

Our midday break at the Armstrong-Kelley Park brought with it additional walkers: my and Marie's brother, Steve, his spouse, Jillian, and my niece, Laurel; and Cape Cod poet, Wilderness Sarchild, for her first of four walks. This was a much-needed rest stop after hours in the rain and humidity, and a heartwarming assembly—for the first time of that summer, my entire immediate family was walking with me.

Over the past several years, and in particular over the course of the spring of 2020 with the multiple deaths of Black people by the police, our biracial family had engaged in deep, challenging, and sometimes painful conversations about race and white supremacy in America. Little did we know then what lay ahead for the next six months—the Black Lives Matter protests, the election, and the insurrection at the Capitol in January 2021. For that day, my family was there to support my journey of understanding social justice on Cape Cod, and I was thrilled to see them during the pandemic summer.

Over fruit and juices, we paid tribute to **John Lewis,** the civil rights legend, Georgia Representative, and Democratic Party leader in Congress who passed away that week. I shared two poignant quotes from Rep. Lewis:

*"**You are a light.** You are the light. Never let anyone—any person or any force—dampen, dim or diminish your light.... Release the need to hate, to harbor division, and the enticement of revenge. Release all bitterness. Hold only love, only peace in your heart, knowing that the battle of good to overcome evil is already won."*

"...ours is not the struggle of one day, one week, or one year. Ours is not the struggle of one judicial appointment or presidential term. Ours is the struggle of a lifetime, or maybe even many lifetimes, and each one of us in every generation must do our part."

We then read a poem about the Covid-19 crisis by **Nikkiesha McLeod,** my sister-in-law's sister, a Black poet and musician in New York City who was with us in spirit that day:

Missing: Corona Diaries

Summer nights, when the air is perfumed with barbecue, and peppered with a gamut of sounds blasting from windows and speeding cars. The chatter of get togethers with the occasional scandalous uproar of laughter. Summer nights, that sizzles with heat even after the sun sets, mosquitoes mark us in our sluttish outfits. We cool off while smelling like the sweltering outside, which dreams and longs for a breeze to soothe the thickness of the atmosphere. We used to gather with our homemade delicacies given as an offering, a ritual of the time welcoming a blaze of fireflies saying good evening.

We walked on through Centerville to Craigville Beach Rd, with different conversations springing up among the various group members, including my 5-year-old niece. We supported each other's quest for engagement with the path we were walking and the people we were with. We walked by some of the most expensive real estate on the Cape, mansions and acres of property that abutt Nantucket Sound and is cared for by an army of landscapers and caretakers in matching shirts.

At one point we stopped in a driveway to take a water break. A landscaper from across the street came over to us and asked what we were doing. There we were, a group of five white women, one white man, one Black woman, and her biracial child. Why was someone crossing the street to ask us what we were doing there? Did he want to provide us directions or assistance? Three of us had on the purple Cape Cod Camino Way tee shirt. We looked like a walking group. I thought it was "no big deal." My brother questioned his motive on behalf of the group, and his wife. He later told me that they are used to being questioned, to being seen as "different." **This happens to them, and other multiracial families, all the time—being asked why they're walking in an upscale neighborhood.** We had just been profiled, and I wasn't aware it was happening. I walked on in silence, feeling some measure of shame, thinking about how the interaction impacted him and my sister-in-law differently than me, and wondering what I could do differently in the future to interrupt the microaggression.

Stopping at the beach to refresh and pick up another walker, Linda, we made our way for the next 3 miles into Hyannis. I pointed out the Craigville Retreat Center where the Methodist campground evolved over the years into a large community extending across Cape Cod and Martha's Vineyard that offers camps, conferences, and retreats.

It was at the Center that we saw, for the first time that day, a few **Black Lives Matter signs.** What did this mean? Why had we not seen them while passing through the other towns? Why did we see Ron Beaty (an outspoken Republican and then-Barnstable County Commissioner) signs back in Marstons Mills with "BLM" spray-painted on them? A few of us acknowledged the level of discourse on Cape Cod, was fractured and angry in tone. We agreed that we are no different than the rest of the country. This led us to several questions: When is anger justified? When is civil disobedience?

The final stop on Walk 3 turned out to be the highlight of the day: the **Zion Union Heritage Museum** tour with **John Reed, the Executive Director, Pamela Chatterton-Purdy, the creator of the *Icons of the Civil Rights Movement*, and Rev. Dr. David A. Purdy, a Member of the Board.** A few others joined us for the tour, including Falmouth student Lilli Feronti (who provided social media coverage for the Camino Way) and Kathleen Schatzberg, former President of Cape Cod Community College. Our group of walkers were provided a history of the founding of the Museum and the story behind the creation of the Icons, including the latest Icon of Trayvon Martin. John Reed, also President of the local chapter of the NAACP, shared stories of the experiences of people of color on Cape Cod, in particular in the Hyannis region.

The same issues we read about daily in the national news were also found here on the Cape: Black people being stopped by the police for no reason. Black people being followed in stores. Black people not on Rt. 6A after dark. I had never heard of that last particular concern before, but the more I thought about it, the more it made sense. These issues of justice, economics, and health care were told with emotion and conviction as we sat and listened in the church pews.

Pamela's personal story was moving—that of a white couple with biracial and Black children. She went into detail about the abuse her son suffered from white children and the education system. In telling her story, she used the offensive "N-word," and I remember cringing and glancing around the room. Later, my sister-in-law would share with me how hurt and offended she was to hear that word in front of her 5-year-old daughter. Again, something landed on her during our experience there much differently than it landed on me. I was grateful for the work we have done together as a family that made her feel comfortable sharing her reflections with me. This is how we grow, individually and together.

After the talk, several of us engaged with John and Pamela about the connections of the art in the museum to the current Black Lives Matter movement and the racial justice issues playing out across the country. **Pamela's Icons of the Civil Rights Movement, 40 painted icons that portray people and events of importance in Black history and civil rights, are extraordinary.** They include former President Barack Obama, Rep. John Lewis, Harriet Tubman, Fannie Lou Hamer, Sojourner Truth, and Trayvon Martin.

One icon represents **Boyrereau Brinch, a former enslaved man more widely known as Jeffrey Brace, who secured his freedom after fighting in the Revolutionary War**, and later relayed his memoirs to be published as *The Blind African Slave or the Memoirs of Boyrereau Brinch, Nicknamed Jeffrey Brace.* My childhood neighbors across the street in Springfield, the Brace family, had traced their family lineage to him in the 1700s. My family and I attended a talk given by my neighbor, Rhonda Brace, about her family tree when the icons were on loan to the Springfield Museums in 2017, and learned that Jeffrey Brace's great-grandson, Peter Brace, had served in the Civil War in the African-American 54th Regiment from Massachusetts. My mother and her mother had shared many an afternoon in the 1960s and '70s raising their children and trying to see the world from each other's eyes.

Pamela Chatterton-Purdy, *Jeffrey Brace FROM SLAVE SHIP TO FREEDOM* 1742-1827, 30" X 48"
http://www.chatterton-purdyart.com/artwork/jeffrey-brace/

Touched by this childhood connection and moved by Pamela's gorgeous artwork, we purchased her book of the icons and stories, so we could continue to learn about the people and experiences of Black culture she represented in her work.

Most Cape Codders do not know about the Zion Union Heritage Museum, or the contributions of people of color to art and culture on Cape Cod. I was personally drawn to the work of resident artist **Robin Joyce Miller**, who **chronicles the life of African Americans from the "Middle Passage" to the inauguration of President Barack Obama.** Her use of the traditional medium of **quilting is a natural a tapestry for storytelling,** and her interpretations of Langston Hughes' poetry is particularly stunning.

Robin Joyce Miller, Inauguration Day Quilt, https://robinjoycemillerart.com/gallery/rhythms-of-a-faithful-journey-collection/

Several members of our group were drawn to the vibrant works of **Carl Lopes**. His paintings pay respect to centuries of influential African design and tradition. **His colors, patterns, and compositions pay tribute to ancestral heritages and cultures, yet maintain a direct contemporary vibe.** Masks, portraits, birds, and fish are embellished with geometric motifs and designs that visually pop.

Outside the Museum, I asked the day's walk participants, **"What inspires you to continue to learn the story of people of color on Cape Cod? What is a key takeaway for you?"** Here are a few of their edited comments:

- "I want to understand the perspective of people of color."
- "I had no idea of the richness of the art contained at the museum."
- "I want to know more. We all need to know more."
- "Walking from the Wampanoag Museum to Zion was a true pilgrimage, highlighting hundreds of years of transgressions against BIPOC."
- "I want to share these stories with other white friends on the Cape so they will come to appreciate the contributions of people of color."

"For me, the walks were an opportunity to learn about BIPOC's contributions to the Cape and all of society and, also, racial injustice from the perspective of each town on the Cape that we walked through. I especially loved visiting the Zion Union African American Museum for the culture, art and history that was beautifully represented. Learning that there was chattel slavery on in Brewster shocked me, and inspired me to join a reparations task force sponsored by First Parish Brewster.

It was gratifying to share several of the walks with my 13 year old granddaughter, who is taking this learning into her social circles and her school projects. I loved walking with like-minded people who are committed to ending racial injustice locally and in the wider world."

-Wilderness Sarchild, Wellfleet

I want to note, my sister Marie provided the logistical support to our walkers that day. I am grateful that my immediate family joined me for a truly inspiring walk. I also want to thank Lauren, who came along for the third time and braved the rain for over an hour on busy stretches of Routes 130 and 28. Thanks to everyone who participated and made this a special day for our family!

Resources:

Across That Bridge: A Vision for Change and the Future of America by John Lewis

Globalcitizen.org - Information on John Lewis and 12 Black activists and authors providing crucial insight into racial justice in the U.S.

Journeys in the Light: Untold Stories of Cape Cod, A documentary of the stories of people of color on Cape Cod: DVD available at the Zion Union Heritage Museum

Mashpee Wampanoag Indian Museum
https://mashpeewampanoagtribe-nsn.gov/museum

Zion Union Heritage Museum: A Museum of History / A Museum of Art Celebrating the Contributions of African-Americans, Cape Verdeans, and Native Americans

zuhmi.org

Create Your Own Walk with Friends and Family

The route from Mashpee through Centerville, Osterville, Barnstable, and Hyannis does not lend itself neatly to an extended walk due to the lack of sidewalks along much of the route. The following options provide an educational and outdoor experience open to all abilities:

Option 1: Park at Mashpee Community Garden and walk to the Wampanoag Museum on Route 130. You can visit the outdoor exhibits if the museum is not open. Go to the museum's website to read and discuss the history of the Wampanoag peoples, their culture, and writings. Share with each other thoughts about the wetu structure behind the museum and the history of their nomadic lifestyle. Continue on Route 130, turn left onto Lake Ave, and continue on to Mashpee River Dam and Attaquin Park. Return to Route 130 and turn left, then left again on Fisherman's Landing and to the water. – 1-2 miles

Option 2: For a longer walk in Hyannis, start at the John F. Kennedy Hyannis Museum on Main St next to the Post Office. Give yourself enough time to take in the JFK Museum (allow for at least one hour) and enjoy the interesting exhibits and photos. Follow Ocean St to the Harbor, then out to the John F. Kennedy Memorial and the Korean War Memorial at Veterans Memorial Park. Take Gosnold St to turn right on Sea St back through town, then left on North St to end at the Zion Union Heritage Museum. – 3 miles

Option 3: For a shorter Hyannis walk, start at the John F. Kennedy Museum on Main St, walk to Sea St, then turn left on North St to end at the Zion Union Heritage Museum. – 1.5 miles

For a Hyannis walk, I suggest focusing your time on the history and culture of people of color on Cape Cod by timing your visit to the hours that the Zion Union Heritage Museum is open. Leave at least 1.5 hours to tour the museum and discuss the exhibits, vibrant artwork, interesting artifacts, repurposed church, and icons depicting historically and culturally significant Black people and events. Interact with each other while viewing the icons. What stories are new to you? Why have we not learned about these important people and events in school? What can you do to continue to educate yourself about Black culture, history, and art?

Discuss the impact of the Kennedy family and their legacy regarding civil rights. Consider the entire Kennedy legacy: JFK, Bobby Kennedy, Eunice Kennedy Shriver, Ted Kennedy, and the current generation of Kennedys. Use the resources available on the museum's website or through your tour to discuss how one family played such an important role in civil rights and social justice movements in the U.S.

Walk 4
Walking the Bay Side –
Economic and Justice Issues

"Walking to explore issues of racism on Cape Cod, especially stopping at the James Baldwin mural and the Barnstable Courthouse was powerful. I also enjoyed hearing about what a strong woman Mercy Otis Warren was. The walks are a great way to talk with others about challenging topics."

-Licia Fields, *Walk 4 Participant*

July 29, 2020

Towns: Barnstable, Yarmouth Port, Dennis

Route: From YMCA Cape Cod in Barnstable along the north side of the Old King's Highway/Route 6A, with detours on side roads. Detour onto Keveney Ln to Mill Ln, Water St, Wharf Ln, and onto Thatcher Shore Rd back to 6A. Detour onto Canterbury Rd to Cromwell Dr, left on Collingwood Dr, right on Sheltered Hollow Ln, and left on Bray Farm Rd S to visit the Taylor-Bray Farm, then continue on Bray Farm Rd N, turn right on Embassy Ln, and left on Longfellow Dr to return to 6A. Follow 6A all the way to the Cape Cod Museum of Art. – 11 miles
NOTE: Parts of 6A have inadequate or no sidewalks.

Sites:
- Cape Cod Community College
- Cape Symphony
- Historic District of Route 6A
- Barnstable Historical Society
- *Baldwin on the Barn* mural
- Barnstable District Court
- Mercy Otis Warren statue
- Taylor-Bray Farm
- Association to Preserve Cape Cod
- Cape Abilities
- Cape Cod Center for the Arts complex

Issues Explored:
- Education on the Cape
- Economic issues on the Cape: housing, childcare, food security, jobs
- Policing and Black Lives Matter's call to "defund the police"
- Climate change and preservation issues
- The Arts (music, theater, museums) and their connections to BIPOC artists and themes

The fourth walk started at the YMCA Cape Cod parking lot on Iyannough Rd/Rt 132 in Barnstable, across from **Cape Cod Community College** (CCCC). Lauren and my friend Licia joined me that day. Licia, a massage therapist from Brewster, and I were part of a group of white women who met over the winter and spring of 2020 to read *White Fragility* by Robin DiAngelo to unpack privilege and racism. A dedicated activist, Licia continues to inspire others by modeling social justice practices in her life. (And she's a great vegan chef!)

We met at the College at 7:30 A.M., an earlier start time due to the heat, noticed the preparations for the day program at the YMCA, and wondered about the economics of childcare in the pandemic. None of us had children of our own. We wondered who must continue to work every day, with or without the appropriate support for children? We recognized that we were privileged to be walking mid-week without demanding family obligations to navigate around.

Our focus today was on the Cape Cod economy and justice issues for people of color on the Cape. When mapping out the route I noticed that we would pass many historical markers on Rt 6A, and planned to stop and discuss whatever we saw along the way. I wanted to make connections between the history we would see and the societal issues we currently face on the Cape, in Massachusetts, and across the country. We each set an intention and honored the land of the Native Americans that we would travel that day.

Earlier in the month, I had spoken with Arlene Rodriguez, the Vice President for Academic & Student Affairs at Cape Cod Community College about resources available to support students during the pandemic. I also read the editorial in the *Cape Cod Times* by CCCC President John Cox encouraging students to consider the economics of remaining at home and enrolling at CCCC for the fall semester. Many college students were considering the options of remaining at home for the fall semester of 2020, or taking a gap year to help manage the disruptions of the pandemic. Both VP Rodriguez and President Cox spoke about the mandate of the community college system to provide an excellent, supportive environment for the approximately 3,000 students that attend their college each semester. Students of color comprise approximately 25% of the population at the college, and can use it as a gateway to a four-year degree. CCCC also provides a food pantry for students with food insecurity, and offers specific services for members of the military, veterans, and students with economic challenges. As we walked by their campus, we reflected on the temporary and lasting effects the pandemic's disruption has caused for CCCC's students and its community.

Before leaving the Route 132 neighborhood, we acknowledged the outstanding leadership Artistic Director and Conductor Jung-Ho Pak provides for the Cape Symphony and its Conservatory down the street. In the winter of 2020, Licia and I attended the Symphony program *Passport to Africa*, an authentic and powerful experience of African music showcasing original works by African composers and musicians. Jung-Ho is an inspirational and innovative leader, taking risks to bring musical variety to the Cape in order to both provide enjoyment and to broaden his audience's exposure to new work. The Cape Symphony had to postpone its 2020 "Mayflower 400" premier events—two new works commissioned in partnership with Plymouth Philharmonic that commemorate the signing of the Mayflower Compact and the stories of the Wampanoag people living here when the Pilgrims' arrived. The program will feature Native singer Jonathan Perry, soprano Kristin Watson, and Wampanoag performers. I hope to attend this program in 2021!

> I highly recommend watching Jung-Ho Pak's inspiring talk at the Cape Cod Museum of Art in 2016, TO BE OR NOT TO BE? The survival of the arts in a Netflix economy, available on their website at: www.ccmoa.org/on-demand-videos

The Old King's Highway, Route 6A, is the largest continuous historic district in the nation. We joined 6A in Barnstable, walking through some of the oldest towns on Cape Cod, with many homes, cemeteries, public buildings, and historical places to visit along the way. We walked by the Olde Colonial Courthouse and the **Lothrop Hill Cemetery**, one of the oldest cemeteries on the Cape, with one grave dated 1643. Two of the historical markers we passed include:

"1639
At this rock now in fragments tradition reports
that the Settlers of Barnstable received the
sacrament for the first time in their new abode
and held their first town meeting."

I was struck that the plaque's wording of the Pilgrims' "new abode," when they had actually been colonizing lands that belonged to the Native peoples.

"In honor of the Men of Barnstable who
served in the Revolution, The War of 1812,
The Civil War, The War with Spain, The War
with Germany..."

Behind this rock stood a "Standing in Solidarity Black Lives Matter" sign. We commented on the juxtaposition of history and current issues displayed in these two signs. We would see many more examples like this on our walks over the course of the summer.

In a stretch of about 100 yards, we saw the following along Old King's Highway: **Saint Mary's Episcopal Church Barnstable**, complete with a rainbow flag affirming designation; a "Together We Rise" sign; and an "Every Vote Counts" sign by the League of Women Voters of the Cape Cod Area. We thought about how some areas on Cape Cod are more liberal, and others lean more conservative. How do people join in conversations across differences? How does where you live, worship, and attend school matter? We all thought that it does matter, and reflected on our own experiences of the neighborhoods where we grew up, the schools we attended, the churches and other social organizations we were members of. All of that mattered a great deal in the formation of who we are today. We also acknowledged how the economic and social structures on the Cape historically and currently prevent people of color from economic prosperity and justice.

The disproportionate number of people of color in the service industries on the Cape (i.e., tourism, healthcare) continues to restrict economic mobility. Because of this, many people of color continued to work in public-facing service roles throughout the pandemic, thereby being exposed to hazards that white-collar employees who can work remotely do not have to risk.

At the **Sturgis Library** we encountered a charming display of a children's book, *RAIN!*, written by Linda Ashman and illustrated by Christian Robinson, on posters out front. We were all impressed with the multicultural families represented in its story. I feel that it's important for not only children of color to see themselves represented in the media they consume, but also for all children to be exposed to stories and understanding of children different from themselves. I congratulate the excellent public libraries on Cape Cod that continue to provide needed contemporary services while preserving and promoting the history of Cape Cod.

Across from Sturgis we found the latest artistic addition to the Old King's Highway: the **James Baldwin Mural** that was painted on the side of a privately-owned carriage house that summer as part of the rising social justice movement. The mural, titled *Baldwin on the Barn*, was created by Cape Cod artists, Joe Diggs and Jackie Reeves. It quotes Baldwin, **"Not everything that is faced can be changed, but nothing can be changed until it is faced."** The mural has been controversial to some because of regulations in the historic district governing building paint colors and signage, and to others because of the quote itself.

We couldn't help thinking that the mural is also provocative to some because it depicts the face of a prominent Black male, James Baldwin, and a challenge to the status quo. David Munsell Jr., the owner of the property with his wife, Diane Griffin Munsell, was quoted in the *Cape Cod Times* when asked why they commissioned the work: **"It's an opportunity to learn and look at things from a different perspective."**

We sat on the library's stone wall across from the mural for a break, and thought about how to raise our voices, how to challenge established rules and norms. Who gets to make the rules and tell the story? How could we be more influential right here on the Cape through (and within) the various organizations where we already spend our time?

What followed was a spirited, and sometimes tense, discussion of when it is appropriate to destroy property in the name of protest. In the example of defacing the sign of a candidate's running for office, I said I did not believe it was right. In a democracy, I would like to see all the signs, take in a variety of forms of media, and make up my mind on a candidate. Free speech, including advertising for elected office, should be a protected right. One person disagreed and argued that until the playing field is equal, all measures of protest, including destruction of property, was within bounds. She also expressed that because I didn't experience the threat of violence that people of color have had to live with, perhaps it explained why the destruction of property appeared an "extreme" measure to me. I became tense and uncomfortable. I did a lot of thinking about the issue of destruction of property during the protests in the spring and summer of 2020. Although I intellectually understand why some people blocked access to roads as a form of protest, or destroyed property, I continued to struggle with destructive or disruptive protests as a normative and appropriate response. Ironically, for three decades in my past career, I advised and assisted students at several colleges to raise their voices and protest various policies and issues. My perspective on protest activity has been shaped by both my family background (working class, white, Catholic), and by this experience as a higher education administrator charged with enforcing the codes of student conduct on college campuses. My training as a yoga teacher, mediator, and coach also contributes to my resistance to the destruction of property as a form of protest.

While sitting on the wall and reflecting on my associations with destruction of property, I recalled three memories, incidents I've held in my mind and body all my life, of being robbed (once as a child, once as a teenager, and once as a college student). I shared this remembrance with my two friends walking with me that day. Why did these memories come flooding back to me as I sat across from the Baldwin memorial, participating in a discussion about violence?

Why did I feel the tension in my body remembering my family of six being assaulted and robbed in Boston as we dropped my brother off at college? What did it mean to experience that fear 40 years ago and walk this pilgrimage today? Was it because all the incidents involved Black men, and I was looking across at a Black male painted on the barn? There are connections across the decades embedded in my psyche and body that I need to continue to examine, contextualize, and heal from. I asked my friends walking with me to resist making assumptions about the experiences of people we encounter. We don't know what resides in people's life stories until we listen to each other, reflect on what is being communicated, and come to understand another person fully. Being open to listening was one of the reasons I developed the Camino Way, a walk across Cape Cod to learn about its current issues of racial and social justice.

Our next stop was the steps of the **Barnstable Courthouse** for a focus on the **policing** of people of color, and to honor Mercy Otis Warren of the American Revolutionary era. In an article of the *Cape Cod Times* in June 2020, the Cape Cod police chiefs called the murder of George Floyd brutal, saying it should never have happened. "I was horrified by what I saw," Brewster Chief Heath Eldredge stated, "It's not what we train our officers to do." Chief Frank Frederickson from Yarmouth hosted a meeting between the Cape's chiefs and the Barnstable County Human Rights Advisory Commission to discuss policing on the Cape. Frederickson said he did not see the Floyd incident as having to do with race.

"We don't even look at this as a racial incident for the most part. We see a human being, getting knelt on and murdered. It didn't matter what color that person was. We just saw a human being murdered by a police officer. That's disgusting." (*Cape Cod Times*, June 4, 2020) Ethan Genter reported that "he said he understood the *perception* that it was racially motivated." John Reed, President of the Cape Cod chapter of the NAACP and Director of the Zion Union Heritage Museum, with whom we'd met the prior week, disagreed and labeled the incident as "clearly racial." I was again struck by the synchronicity of meeting Mr. Reed one week, and reading his response to the police chief's dismissal of George Floyd's death as not "racially motivated" the next. John was right, as were the activists all over the country who clearly saw the power of white privilege acted out in the murder of George Floyd. We were frustrated and angry by the response of our local police. The police needed to be held accountable to this and so many other deaths of Black and Brown people.

I read excerpts from an op-ed in the *Boston Globe* (May 28, 2019) written by Michael O'Keefe, five term District Attorney for the Cape and Islands, criticizing the "social justice" platform of Rachael Rollins, the DA for Suffolk County. Rollins, who happens to be the only Black and female DA in the state, said her office will not prosecute low-level offenders, instead helping them to access assistance needed through social systems. Rollins told O'Keefe to focus on his own county. In a collection of response letters, Stephanie Roberts Hartung, a former public defender and current professor at Northeastern University School of Law, accuses him of a "thinly veiled racist" attack by referencing his argument that the "'disintegration of the family,' 'lack of respect for discipline in education,' and 'the glorification in some communities of a culture that celebrates disrespectful language and misogyny under the guise of art'" are the causes of the disparate rate of prosecution and incarceration of Black and Latino men. We agreed that our prison systems are filled with Black and Brown men, many in need of social services and economic opportunities rather than prison sentences. As we learned more about the "defund the police" initiative, I acknowledged that I struggled with the slogan and hoped something less polarizing could be created for this initiative. I understood that the police currently serve the function of various social service agencies though they are neither trained nor equipped to do so, and that this system must change. But I was not ready to fully embrace the "defund the police" campaign if it was interpreted as moving to eliminate all policing functions.

We kept these thoughts on policing in mind as we sat at the foot of the **Mercy Otis Warren** (1728–1814) statue on the courthouse lawn, and honored her role as a political writer, propogandist, and political activist during the American Revolution and early years of the republic. She became a correspondent and advisor to many political leaders, including Samuel Adams, John Hancock, Patrick Henry, Thomas Jefferson, George Washington, and especially John Adams, who encouraged her to use her voice in the pollical process. Mercy was educated alongside her brothers and devoured books, learning history and language, and becoming a gifted writer. She broke many traditional gender roles of her time and continues to serve as an inspiration for us today. I noted to the group that this was the third statue of a woman we'd passed on our walks so far (after Katharine Lee Bates' statue in Falmouth and Rachel Carson's in Woods Hole). I wondered how many others are on Cape Cod?

We continued up Route 6A and passed the **Coast Guard Heritage Museum** (which was closed) where I had hoped to stop to honor my sister-in-law who is a faculty member at the USCG Academy. Last year, the Coast Guard celebrated the 40th anniversary of women graduating from the Academy, though like the other branches of the military, it continues to struggle with issues of race and gender.

Across the street, the **Unitarian Church of Barnstable** displayed a large Black Lives Matter sign out front as well as advertised the continuation of their inspirational events online. A short way up the road, across from the Cape Cod Organic Farm, we found a wonderful sign depicting two hands entwined that read: **"I understand that I will never understand. However, I stand with you."** This sign summed up that day for me, as well as the overall purpose behind my walks and conversations!

Slightly further down the road we passed a sign denoting the gravesite of **Iyanough**, a sachem and leader of the Mattachiest tribe (a subgroup of the Wampanoag people) of Cummaquid in the area of present-day Barnstable. The village of Hyannis and the Wianno district of Osterville are named after Iyanough. Numerous Native American names grace our towns, streets, ponds, and other places on Cape Cod, and we sought to recall them as we walked up the winding road.

We took a detour off 6A and followed the narrow lanes down to the Bass Hole boardwalk over the Grays Beach marsh looking out to Barnstable Harbor. On the way back we bought fresh produce at Cape Cod Organic's farm stand, and ate the just-picked green beans right from the bag—we needed that refreshment!

At the historic town center of Yarmouth, Lauren took us behind the Captain Bangs Hallet House Museum to see an amazing tree specimen—**a giant, 120-year-old weeping beech tree** supposedly possessing magical powers. We paused to honor this ancient tree and be blessed in her presence. We then discovered a sand sculpture of the Mayflower amidst these historic Yarmouth houses. And there we were again: at the striking juxtaposition of nature and humanmade forms of art. And the Pilgrims continued to stalk us along our way. We continued along 6A with no sidewalk and the traffic bearing down on us in the severe heat. Even with the two gallons of water I brought with me, I was parched and light-headed, so we stopped for provisions and a break in the shade. We detoured off 6A again to take in the vista at Taylor-Bray Farm, and learned of its ongoing excavation of Native American artifacts dating back 10,000 years. I returned to the Farm several times over the summer to better understand this history and share it with others who came to visit me.

We were happy to reach **Cape Abilities**, a nonprofit organization that provides jobs, homes, transportation, and social and therapeutic services for people with disabilities across Cape Cod. Both Lauren and I had been to Cape Abilities many times and support their services regularly. Next door on 6A resides the **Association to Preserve Cape Cod (APCC)**, the regional conservation organization with a focus on climate change, sustainability, water quality, and habitat protection. APCC is the leading environmental voice in the region, ever-vigilantly opposing environmental protection rollbacks by the federal government, and supporting development of offshore wind. Resources on their website include fact sheets, maps, presentations, videos, and reports for the general public's reference and use. Executive Director **Andrew Gottlieb** has become an outspoken advocate for the environment, having challenged many actions of the Trump Administration, and his thought-provoking blog on the APCC website, *What I'm Thinking*, is a must-read. Here's a few quotes from his June 3, 2020 entry:

> *"...After spending Monday night watching my government disperse peaceful, yes peaceful, protesters with flash grenades, tear gas and rubber bullets just to enable a cynical and shameful photo-op, some things became clear. As a nation we are pulled toward authoritarianism. This isn't hyperbole or speculation; it is not typical election year posturing or anything else even vaguely normal or acceptable in modern America. But it is right there, out in the open and there for all to see. We are witnessing the power of the federal government being turned on the people it was elected to serve."*

> *"No one knows where this stops if we don't take action. While as individuals we might feel our voice doesn't matter, the collective voice has always been the guiding light behind positive change and justice in America."*

Another of his blog entries examines the pandemic's significant effect on Cape Cod: more people working and living here year-round; second homes becoming first homes; remote learning; and the migration of city-dwellers challenging our educational and natural resources. There have also been changes to our seasonal economy, housing market, and rental availability. And the Cape will continue to feel the effects of the pandemic through 2021 in the differences felt in its aging population and the changes in economic opportunities for seasonal workers and people of color.

We ended our walk at the grounds of the **Cape Playhouse and Cape Cod Museum of Art**. We noted that although neither venue was open, the Museum would open soon with a new show, *Journey: A Mayflower 400 Project*, as part of the scheduled 2020 Mayflower anniversary celebrations. I looked forward to returning to the museum to see the show and consider all aspects of the 400th anniversary of the journey of the Pilgrims to Cape Cod. We toured the outdoor sculpture garden, a welcome shady place to take in the outstanding artwork by Cape Cod artists, including several depictions of women and feminine themes.

The Cape Playhouse's website explained that their planned 2020 Season of such classics as *Grease*, *Murder on the Orient Express*, and *An American in Paris* were postponed to the summer of 2021. I hoped the Playhouse would use their venue and status as a leading theater on the Cape to explore current issues related to social and racial justice. Live theater is such a powerful way to experience challenging and thought-provoking topics in a small setting, and I hoped that Cape theaters would lead the way.

After the walk on my drive back to Brewster, I took one more detour to investigate a sign I had driven by hundreds of times on 6A in Dennis that reads, **"Burial Ground of the Nobscussett Tribe of Indians of which tribe Mashantampaine was chief."** Bordering Scargo Pond, I'd found a site infused with sacred spirit. What a gem! I was honored to spend some time at this special place, surrounded by numerous artifacts like flags, shells, dolls, stone markers, etc. This special stop reminded me again that when you pass a sign that piques your interest, definitely stop and investigate!

Walk Four was in the books. I was halfway through my journey across Cape Cod, and was thrilled to be undertaking this pilgrimage during the pandemic summer. I could think of no better way to spend my summer of 2020 than walking, experiencing, and learning about the lives and stories of all people on Cape Cod.

Resources:

Association to Preserve Cape Cod
https://apcc.org/
Mercy Otis Warren, Barnstable County
https://www.barnstablecounty.org/affiliated-organizations/mercy-otis-warren-woman-year/
Barnstable Historical Society
https://barnstablehistoricalsociety.org/
Cape Abilities
https://www.capeabilities.org/
Cape Cod Museum of Art
https://www.ccmoa.org/
Coast Guard Heritage Museum
https://coastguardheritagemuseum.org/
Cape Playhouse
https://www.capeplayhouse.com/
Cape Symphony
https://www.capesymphony.org/
Taylor-Bray Farm
https://www.taylorbrayfarm.org/

Create Your Own Walk with Friends and Family

Option 1: For a **shorter version** of this walk (approximately 3 miles), park at the Sturgis Library on Route 6A and visit the Barnstable Historical Society, next to the *Baldwin on the Barn* mural. Reflect on what it means to have current social justice issues depicted so prominently on a building in a historic district. What is free speech in our country and how does it play out for different groups of people?

Walk up 6A to the Barnstable Courthouse and reference the Barnstable County website for information about Mercy Otis Warren and her impact on the American Revolution. Consider the current issues around policing on Cape Cod as well as across the country. What needs to continue to change to eliminate bias in policing? And what larger societal structures need to change to end systemic racism in our criminal justice system?

Continue on 6A to the Coast Guard Heritage Museum, taking in the exhibits if they are open. Then backtrack to turn right on Millway and continue to Barnstable Harbor Ecotours and the whale watcher cruises at the harbor. Consider the pandemic's impact on the commercial industries at Mattakeese Wharf and spend some time learning about the history of the area from the Barnstable Historical Society website.

Option 2: For a **longer walk,** take Commerce Rd back to 6A and enjoy views of Maraspin Creek, then return to Sturgis library. You will pass many stores and shops on 6A for provisions.

Consider driving up the road to the Captain Bangs Hallet House Museum in Yarmouth and its large weeping beech tree. And a visit to Taylor-Bray Farm is an opportunity to picnic on the grounds. Finally, if driving, continue up 6A to the Cape Cod Museum of Art and the Nobscussett Indian Burial Ground. You will not be disappointed!

Walk 5
Focus on Health – Mind/Body/Spirit

> *"We learn by going where we have to go; we arrive when we find ourselves on the road walking toward us."*
>
> -Phil Cousineau, *The Art of Pilgrimage: The Seeker's Guide to Making Travel Sacred*

August 5, 2020

Towns: Dennis, Harwich, Chatham

Route: Cape Cod Rail Trail from Dennis to Atwood House Museum – 14.5 miles

Sites:

- Pilgrim's Landing
- Chase Park
- Chatham Labyrinth
- Atwood Museum and Wampanoag Wetu

Issues Explored:
- Cape Cod Healthcare and Covid-19's disproportionate impact on BIPOC
- Cape Verdeans and the cranberry industry
- Wellness: Mind, Body, and Spirit

We began at 7:30 a.m. at the start of the Cape Cod Rail Trail in Dennis on Route 134. Lauren was reliably present again, and Rita, a nurse in the Providence public schools, left Rhode Island very early to join us. I met Rita in the fall of 2019 at a writer's workshop at Kripalu, the yoga and holistic health retreat center in the Berkshires. I knew she cared about social justice issues and I welcomed the idea of having someone with a healthcare background join us on this leg of the journey. Both Lauren and I have developed a yoga and meditation practice, which we wove into our walking experience each week. These walks were providing a rich mind/body/spirit opportunity, touching on all aspects of physical, psychological, and spiritual health.

We started with setting our intentions for the day: to focus on all aspects of health and the disproportionate impacts of racism on the healthcare model in this country and on the Cape. We honored the lands that belong to the people who came before us, the Wampanoag and other tribes, who keep sacred the earth and nature that supports the health of all peoples. We touched on the disparities in access to healthcare related to race and income, and acknowledged our own privilege within this system, as we walked from Dennis, through Harwich, and on to Chatham.

We shared books and documentaries we had become aware of in the past several months to support our learning about racism. I spoke about a documentary I watched at the Woods Hole Film Festival the prior weekend as an excellent example of what one family can do to bridge the divide across the political differences in this country. *The Reunited States* follows a conservative, white couple and their three children as they travel across the U.S. to have conversations with people holding different perspectives than their own. Along the way they confronted real examples of systemic racism present in America's healthcare, economy, housing, and education systems as well as many more infrastructures. Through their personal connection with people and people's stories, their hearts and minds were changed. They now think of people who hold different opinions as potential "allies," with every person having a role to play in reuniting this country. I was struck by how similar their experience was to my Cape Cod Camino Way project: explore a question, build awareness, seek out information, listen to others, be open to change, and change!

I had two responses to this film—the first was a pair of questions: When were we ever "united?" When were people of color and indigenous peoples ever provided the same opportunities as white people? As we explored in the first walk, the establishment of our democracy included the institution of slavery and the appropriation of lands from the Native Americans through violent means. A Civil War and one hundred years of Jim Crow oppression served to keep white people and people of color "separate but equal," or in segregated situations. Even with the Civil Rights Acts of the 1960s and beyond, we have never been "united." Yet my second response was one of hope: by seeking out information, listening to the stories of people different than ourselves, and being open to change, we can heal and make progress.

The documentary ends with two resources: **Listen First Project** and **Bridge Alliance**, which both seek to continue the work of understanding and bridge building. Consider checking them out!

I also watched two other documentaries that week: *13th* on Netflix and *Slavery by Another Name* on PBS. Both films provide some of the context and history that we need to fully understand the historic and current implications of the institution of slavery and the continued systemic racism in the United States, especially in our criminal justice system. As I continued my walks on Cape Cod, and remained open to the activism happening around the country as well as the resources being made available for learning, I found that each week I could share more observations and suggestions for building awareness with my fellow walkers.

After walking the first four miles in the increasing humidity, we stopped near historic Harwich Center and reviewed information on health disparities for Black, Indigenous and People of Color. I shared that I'd recently had a conversation with **Dr. Kumara Sidhartha** from Cape Cod Healthcare. "Dr Sid," as he is known locally, advocates a plant-based approach with food, helping patients understand that food is medicine and eating healthy supports all aspects of health. He spoke about the social determinants of health, such as housing, employment, health insurance, language barriers, and cultural factors, and how they disproportionately impact the health of people of color. He described the double burden of malnutrition, in which individuals living in a poor community have higher rates of obesity. This stems from the poor nutrients and excess calories in the types of available food for lower income levels, worsened by the socialization to choose high calorie/low quality food. Also at play is sugar's addictive role in American diets, and its negative effects on all aspects of health.

The important information in the below chart provided by Dr. Sidhartha shows how Covid-19 disproportionately impacts all people of color:

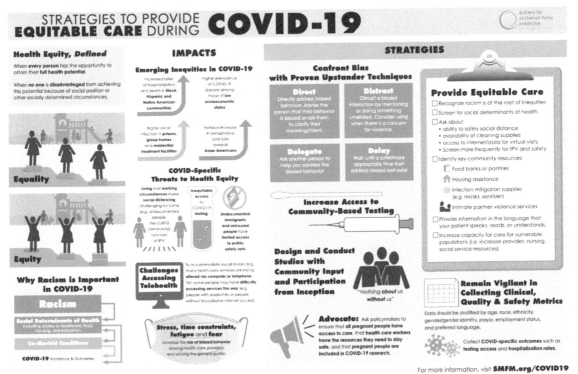

https://s3.amazonaws.com/cdn.smfm.org/media/2385/COVID_Final.pdf

In a short period of time, I found numerous articles and resources that supported Dr. Sid's perspective on these factors impacting health. From the CDC website:

> "*Multiple factors contribute to racial/ethnic health disparities, including socioeconomic factors (e.g., education, employment, and income), lifestyle behaviors (e.g., physical activity and alcohol intake) ...and access to preventative health-care services (e.g., cancer screening and vaccination). Recent immigrants also can be at increased risk for chronic disease and injury, particularly those who lack fluency in English and familiarity with the U.S. health-care system.*"

Upon reading this, I immediately thought of the meat packing industry in this country, and the disproportionate number of people of color and recent immigrants who work on the Covid front line in meat processing plants. They are now considered "essential workers." But if our diets reflected a plant-based approach, we could possibly change the "food industrial complex" and its resulting negative impacts on people of color.

One final initiative Dr. Sidhartha shared with me was the "Navigators" who function in the Cape Cod Healthcare model. These staff work with patients to provide information on everything from temporary housing to food insecurity issues and health insurance. They connect patients with all forms of support needed to navigate the bureaucracy surrounding access to resources in order to support all aspects of their health. The Navigators appear to be a critical part of an effective health system, and I hope that all healthcare systems consider a similar model.

The **American College of Physicians** offer much information online about the racial and ethnic disparities in healthcare such as these selections from their 2010 policy paper:

> "*Social determinants of health are a significant source of health disparities among racial and ethnic minorities. Inequities in education, housing, job security, and environmental health must be erased if health disparities are to be effectively addressed.*"

> "*The healthcare delivery system must be reformed to ensure that patient-centered medical care is easily accessible to racial and ethnic minorities and physicians are enabled with the resources to deliver quality care.*"

And here are some statistics from Jamila Taylor's "**Racism, Inequality, and Health Care for African Americans**" (2019):

- Of the more than 20 million people who gained coverage under the Affordable Care Act, 2.8 million of them are African- American. However, the uninsured rate among African Americans is almost 10%.
- The average cost for health care premiums is 9% higher for African Americans, which is especially damaging considering the demographic's income inequality.
- African-American women are three times more likely to die of pregnancy-related causes than white women.
- African Americans are more likely to die from cancer and heart disease than whites, and are at greater risk for the onset of diabetes.
- African American children are ten times more likely to die by gun violence than white children.

As we walked a rural section of Cape Cod from Harwich into Chatham, the three of us reflected on our personal paths through the healthcare system and our privilege as white individuals in mostly middle-class environments with access to high-quality resources. We also thought about our experiences with Covid, and Rita shared the challenges of nursing at inner city schools in Rhode Island with children of color from families without access to quality resources and healthcare.

After walking a few more miles we crossed Depot Rd and came across several cranberry bogs, a horse farm, and the natural setting of Harwich. As noted in earlier walks, the **Cape Verdean** presence on Cape Cod within the cranberry industry was large in the late 19th and early 20th centuries. Cape Verdeans migrated here until 1920s anti-immigration laws stemmed the flow. Settling in East and North Harwich and the Pleasant Lake community, they were fleeing drought and starvation at home and came to the Cape via the packet boats, known locally as the "Brava fleet" after the Island of Brava. Once in the U.S., they experienced racist and anti-immigrant attitudes, but were sought out for their strong work ethic. Eventually the number of descendants of Cape Verdean immigrants on Cape Cod was 10 times the population of Cape Verde itself. Today there is a thriving connection between Cape Verde and Bridgewater State University where I worked part-time. The **Pedro Pires Institute for Cape Verdean Studies** sponsors exchanges for students and professionals, and has hosted all three of its Prime Ministers since its independence from Portugal in 1975.

Returning to our theme of health, the three walkers discussed how we were staying healthy in the time of the pandemic, and the resources available to us. As we were walking through Harwich, I shared a few comments from **Amy GiaQuinto**, the founder of **Personalized Fitness Solutions** in Harwich Port. Amy is an example of a life-long learner, challenging herself and her clients to continue to grow physically, spiritually, and on issues of race and privilege. I interviewed Amy via email earlier in the week and offered a few of her insights:

"This is a stressful time, consciously and sub-consciously, and focusing on self-care through general wellness and exercise is crucial to help manage stress and anxiety. When we exercise our bodies release endorphins which can help bring about feelings of joy, happiness, and general well-being."

"On both a physical and psychological level, a strong core is vital. Your core, made up of not only your abdominal muscles but also your pelvic floor, lower back, and glute muscles, work together as a unit, vital to building a strong foundation. A strong core helps us to feel physically stable and strong, which in turn helps us emotionally feel more in control and empowered."

"There is a lack of understanding and awareness, and it is our job to educate ourselves and to foster change...my hope is that we will all work together for change."

Each week we encountered the presence of the Native Americans who thrived on Cape Cod before the white settlers arrived in the 1600s. As we continued on the bike path into Chatham, I shared some of the rich Wampanoag history and current connections with the new wetu, constructed by Mashpee Wampanoag member David Weeden and his son Attaquin, behind the **Atwood House**. An exhibit running at the time called "The Turning Point" told the story of the Mayflower and the impact the ship's arrival had on the native people living in the Chatham area.

Historic-Chatham.org is rich with information about the history of the Wampanoag. For thousands of years, they lived in this area, staying near the shore during the warmer months and moving inland for cover in the winter, living in wetus similar to the one now found on the Atwood property. Prior to 1712, the town of Chatham was called the village of Monomoit, one of 67 villages of the Wampanoag nation. The current Route 28 was once the walking path for the native peoples to travel between Chatham and what is now Orleans. The people of **Monomoyick** were hunters, farmers, gatherers, and fished the local waters. Their government and community were designed to create a balanced society between the natural world and one another.

The English colonists arrived with a grant from the King to inhabit the land. An uneasy peace existed for many years between the natives and the colonists, living in their separate villages. English men married Wampanoag women, thus starting prominent Cape family lines like the Nickersons. Many of the founders of the town of Chatham were in fact descendants of Native Americans, although not many people claimed that heritage in a positive way until recently. *"They didn't associate themselves with natives because a lot of times it was easier to not be identified as native,"* Weeden said. *"It was an easier life, to be accepted and assimilated if you didn't identify, so that was a factor."* (*Cape Cod Times,* June 9, 2020)

Approaching Chatham center on Route 28, we stopped at **Pilgrim's Landing**, a not-for-profit Interspiritual Life Center working at the intersection of spirituality, education, and social justice. It is also the home of the **Chatham Labyrinth**, created in 2010. Pilgrim's Landing offers year-round educational programming and meaningful experiences for those on a journey toward a more peaceful, compassionate, and just world.

At this point in the day's journey, we were joined by five other walkers, including Wilderness for her second walk, her granddaughter Saffy, as well as Mary Ellen and two members of the social justice group at the Center—Danielle Tolley and Dawn Tolley, founders and family who, with Anne Bonney, gave birth to the Center in 2013. All three founders joined us for an overview of their programs and services, and the connections to racial and social justice we were exploring on our walk. Danielle provided information on the mission and plans for the Center, and Dawn spoke to us about the heart and soul of the Center's current work being done around social justice and resilience.

We then walked together to the **Labyrinth in Chase Park**. Anne helped us understand the meaning behind the Labyrinth, its origins, and some of the benefits of walking the path. She encouraged us to walk both as individuals and as part of a group of seekers for deeper understanding of social justice issues. Anne also shared the following wisdom with us:

- The labyrinth is an ancient pattern found in many cultures around the world. Labyrinth designs were found on pottery, tablets, and tiles that date as far back as 4,000 years. Many patterns are based on spirals and circles mirrored in nature. In Native American culture it is called the Medicine Wheel and Man in the Maze. The Celts described it as the Never Ending Circle. It is also known as the Kabala in mystical Judaism. One feature all labyrinths have in common is that they have one path that winds in a circuitous way to the center.

• Generally there are three stages to the walk: **releasing** on the way in, **receiving** in the center, and **returning** when you follow the return path back out of the labyrinth. **Symbolically, and sometimes actually, you are taking back out into the world that which you have received.**

• There is no right way or wrong way to walk a labyrinth. Use the labyrinth in any way that meets what you need while being respectful of others walking. You may go directly to the center to sit quietly — whatever meets your needs.

We each walked the Labyrinth's circuits at our own pace, joining together for a debrief after. One participant said she didn't know going into the labyrinth that she needed healing, but that is what she felt from the experience. Another shared that even with the distractions from the noise nearby, it was an opportunity to reflect on her life and be grateful. Everyone found it to be a powerful experience, deeply spiritual and moving. Anne shared with us a blessing which included the phrase "May our longing for oneness, our prayers for circles unbroken, be heard and honored here."

Our walk concluded with a visit to the **Atwood Museum** grounds to see the wetu constructed by the Weedens. It is similar to one we saw on Walk 2 at the Mashpee Wampanoag Indian Museum. We made plans to return to Atwood and see the new exhibit on the Mayflower and the connections to the Wampanoag. We then walked the mile back to Pilgrim's Landing via Oyster Pond and relished the Chatham breeze pushing us onward.

I rushed home to participate as a panelist on a Zoom program led by **Marie Younger Blackburn**: Accomplice vs. Ally. Marie is an entrepreneur from Falmouth, the creator of Driven: Cape Cod's Conference for Women, and the host of Conversations that Matter, a twice monthly virtual summit that provides a safe space for conversations about bias, race, and advocacy on Cape Cod. Marie creates space for true dialogue and understanding for people of all backgrounds. Our session that Wednesday focused on how to support people of color as an accomplice and an ally.

I shared how my experience creating the Camino Way was evolving from a personal journey to a shared experience through my writings, videos, and conversations over the summer. Through a variety of mediums and in a variety of spaces, I was sharing the knowledge and skills gained from a summer of walking across Cape Cod being exposed to stories of racial and social justice. My commitment to being both an ally and an accomplice continued to deepen, eventually evolving into writing this memoir of the experience, which will hopefully encourage others to do the same type of work.

Note: I returned to the Atwood Museum a few weeks later and found not only an outstanding exhibit on the Mayflower voyage with a connection to Chatham, and the story of the Wampanoag people living in the area, but also an exhibit on World War II. My father served in the Navy during the war, and was at Omaha Beach on D-Day. I am always moved by the thought of an 18-year-old assuming a fighting position on a boat, surrounded by hundreds of thousands of other young men trying to break the hold of Nazi Germany on Europe.

The exhibit was also deeply powerful to me for another reason: I noticed one of the photos depicted a Black woman as "Rosie the Riveter." Never before had I seen an image of a Black female working in one of the labor roles assumed by women during the War. I commented on the photo to the two men working at the Atwood, including the curator of the exhibit who wasn't aware of the significance of seeing a Black woman in this role. I thanked him for bringing this part of history to light.

"As a career nurse educator, I am forever driven to enhance my understanding of improving our health and enhancing our state of wellness. I signed up assured that this endeavor would be educational (as a lifelong learner), challenging (14 miles), and good for the soul. Hoping to understand more about the state of health care on Cape Cod and how this affects the lives of Cape Codders, what I learned was something more germane to my own well-being. It made for a delightful day and one I will scarcely forget for a long time."

-Rita Kenahan, Little Compton, RI

Resources:
*13*th documentary
http://www.avaduvernay.com/13th
Atwood Museum
https://chathamhistoricalsociety.org/
Bridge Alliance
https://www.bridgealliance.us/
Chatham Labyrinth
https://chathamlabyrinth.com/

"Faith, independence, accountability all intricately linked" by The Most Rev. James F. David
Cape Cod Times, Matters of Faith column, June 28, 2020
(much-needed advice and support for spiritual health!)
http://evensongministries.com/
"Health Disparities Experienced by Black or African Americans --- United States", CDC
https://www.cdc.gov/mmwr/preview/mmwrhtml/mm5401a1.htm#:~:text=Multiple%20factors%20contribute%20to%20racial,racial%2Fethnic%20discrimination%2C%20and%20neighborhood
Historic Chatham
Historic-Chatham.org
Listen First Project
http://www.listenfirstproject.org/
Pilgrim's Landing
https://pilgrimslandingcapecod.org/
The Reunited States documentary
https://reunitedstates.tv/watch
Slavery by Another Name documentary
http://www.pbs.org/tpt/slavery-by-another-name/home/
Veriditas: Inspiring transformation through the labyrinth experience
https://www.veriditas.org/New-to-the-Labyrinth

Create Your Own Walk with Friends and Family

To create a shorter walk of just sites in Chatham (about 3.3 miles), consider parking at any of the public lots on or near the Eldredge Public Library. If open, seek out the historic information at the library on the town of Chatham and the area's connections with the Wampanoag.

Starting on Main St, turn right on Cross St towards Chase Park and the Chatham Windmill and Labyrinth. Pull up the Pilgrim's Landing website and read about labyrinths and their spiritual connections. Then set an intention and slowly walk to the center of the labyrinth, pausing at the center to breathe deeply before walking with a measured pace outward. Encourage children to explore the grounds and labyrinth with quiet and reverence as others may be seeking silence for insights.

NOTE: Cross streets where appropriate to stay on the sidewalks, or walk against the traffic single file, keeping far to the left side of the road.

Return to Cross St and follow to the left onto Stage Harbor Rd, passing the old schoolhouse, and making your way to the Atwood Museum and Chatham Historical Society. Time your visit to include an hour at the Atwood, a museum suitable for all ages.

Follow Stage Harbor to turn left on Bridge St, crossing Mill Pond and following it until you reach the Chatham Lighthouse. Be reminded of the true story behind the famous Coast Guard rescue depicted in the film, *The Finest Hours*. Look out across the street to Lighthouse Beach and the Chatham break (one long barrier beach stretching from Nauset to Chatham), and consider the impact of climate change on the coastline. Then follow Main St north to turn left on Water St and right on School, taking in the historic neighborhood's homes and gardens. Return to Main St and finish your journey with refreshments from any of the wonderful restaurants in town.

Walk 6
Cape Economy and the Institution of Slavery
&
The Environment and the National Seashore

"When I came here the people were extremely sensitive on certain political questions. We were all slaves to slavery.... About 50 active ship masters lived in town then and every one of them sided with the slave interests."

-Cyrus Augustus Bradley, the First Brewster Parish minister from 1851-1857

August 12, 2020

Towns: Brewster, Orleans, Eastham

Route: Starting at Snowy Owl Coffee Roasters in Brewster on Route 6A, walk to the Cape Cod Rail Trail and follow it through Orleans to turn right on Governor Prence Rd in Eastham. Cross Route 6 to walk through Fort Hill to Hemenway Landing, then take Hemenway Rd back to Route 6 and follow to Eastham Windmill Green and Bandstand, then continue on Route 6 to the Cape Cod National Seashore Salt Pond Visitors Center. – 11 miles

Sites:
- Nickerson State Park
- Fort Hill
- Cape Cod National Seashore
- Eastham Windmill

Issues Explored:
- Cape economy and its connections to the institution of slavery
- Brewster sea captains' legacy
- The Environment: climate change, preservation, the National Seashore
- Native Americans and European explorers

We began the day with cups of coffee in the garden area of the Snowy Owl coffee shop on 6A in Brewster. I was thankful that Lauren was joining for her sixth Walk, Licia joined again brought her friend, Ailene, for her first walk, Wilderness and her granddaughter Saffron were joining again, and Mary Ellen, Jennie, and Chris joined us at our day's start in Brewster. That morning, Lauren presented me with a Peace Flag, a newly redesigned version that displays the word "PEACE" on a background of a rainbow that includes multiple shades of skin tone to represent all people. We embraced its connection to the Camino Way walks as one method of promoting a peaceful world. "The mission of the **Rainbow Peace Flag Project** is to extend kindness and caring across national borders, with love that includes people of all sexualities, genders, abilities, religions, races, and cultures, and to condemn acts of violence and hatred, embracing peaceful dialogue instead."

We then set our intentions for why we were walking that day and offered acknowledgement to the Indigenous peoples whose land we would be walking on and through, from Brewster to Orleans, to Eastham. The nine of us gathered to hear about the history of the Cape economy, particularly that of Brewster with its many sea captains of the late 1700s through the 1800s, and their connections to the enslavement of Africans. During the walk, we also spoke about environmental justice topics, from the establishment of the National Seashore to climate change, algae blooms in our ponds, and sustainable practices for healthy living on Cape Cod. These topics were challenging and complex, requiring many stops along the way to share information and our personal reflections on what we were learning and experiencing.

The Cape's connections to the institution of slavery are complex, and particularly difficult for progressive white people to acknowledge and explore. Our work on this walk, as well as moving forward, was to be open to hearing about how the histories of the towns we love and call home were entwined with the practice of enslaving others, and how this benefited Cape Cod, and the entire Northeast, over time. Even if our individual ancestors came here well after the Emancipation Proclamation and the Civil War ended this practice (as mine did from Ireland and Poland in the early 1900s), we share in the history of economic gains made by those who profited from the Triangular Trade of the 1800s.

For me personally, the preparation for this walk proved to be the hardest Camino week of the summer. It challenged my fundamental assumption about Cape Cod and the Northeast as liberal and progressive places where abolitionist leaders fought to eradicate the institution of slavery. I have owned a home in Brewster for twenty years, living here full time for the past seven years. Through my Camino Way journey, I now have a deeper understanding of the way my community and its former leaders (political, religious, social) were complicit in their interactions with the institution of slavery.

The foundation the Cape economy benefited from trade with the Caribbean in a variety of ways, and continues to embody aspects of institutional racism to this day. To be complicit means to be involved with, intentionally or not, an illegal act or wrongdoing. I also now understand more about my own complicity, and therefore was compelled to share what I was finding with others to hopefully create a new and different future.

I explained to the group how the **Triangular Trade system** generally worked in the 18th and 19th centuries using quotes from a Thought Co. article:

"New Englanders traded extensively, exporting many commodities such as fish, whale oil, furs, and rum and followed the following pattern that occurred as follows:

• New Englanders manufactured and shipped rum to the west coast of Africa in exchange for enslaved people.
• The captives were taken on the Middle Passage to the West Indies where they were sold for molasses and money.
• The molasses would be sent to New England to make rum and start the entire system of trade all over again.

In the colonial era, the various colonies played different roles in what was produced and used for trade purposes in this triangular trade. Massachusetts and Rhode Island were known to produce the highest quality rum from the molasses and sugars that had been imported from the West Indies. The distilleries from these two colonies would prove to be vital to the continued triangular trade of enslaved people that was extremely profitable. Virginia's tobacco and hemp production also played a major role as well as cotton from the southern colonies."

The last part of the quote needed repeating for the walkers: the rum from that sugar cane became a mainstay drink for Cape Codders. Back in the 1700s and 1800s, Americans primarily drank beer and rum, or other fermented drinks distilled from fruits to make cider. New England powered the production of rum, which was used to bargain for Africans and delivered those enslaved people to the Caribbean.

To prepare for this walk, I interviewed two local authorities on Brewster's historical connections to the Triangular Trade, and visited two of Brewster's old cemeteries, one behind the Unitarian Church and the other on Lower Rd. I remember walking these cemeteries several times in the past two decades without carefully reading the headstones and thinking about the stories behind them. I noted how many of the families intermarried and created a strong connection for economic, political, and religious continuity in the town. I then drove up Rt 6A to take photos of the numerous sea captain homes, many of which are now historic inns and taverns, and thought about how we continue to benefit from the beauty and charm of our historic town through tourism.

While I was walking one cemetery at sunset, I spoke with **Meadow Dibble**, a former resident of Brewster and a documentarian, who encouraged me to explore the hidden stories in plain view: symbolic graves of sea captains who died and were buried in Africa, Havana, Port-au-Prince, and other Caribbean ports. Meadow, the founder of **The Atlantic Black Box Project**, years ago noticed a man's grave in the Unitarian cemetery that read, "died in Africa 1795." That raised a major question for her: What was he doing there?

Meadow then took on excavating the story of Elijah Cobb, who built the house on Lower Rd where the Brewster Historical Society is now located, and his history with the ship *Ten Brothers*. The captain and crew of *Ten Brothers* spent much of the fall of 1818 in the Gulf of Guinea off the west coast of Africa. In the harbor of Principe, many on the ship contracted yellow fever and died, including Captain Joseph Mayo. Elijah Cobb, a senior member of the crew, sailed the ship back to Boston, stopping at Martinique to unload an unspecified cargo.

When they arrived in Boston in July 1819, they brought yellow fever with them, causing an epidemic in the city. Cobb was charged with being a public health threat and with slave trading, but was eventually cleared of both charges. Meadow noted that 12 years of Cobb's diaries are missing, including many years when he was at sea. She believes his story was a "don't ask, don't tell" story of that time. Meadow's research now extends to the coast of Maine, where she currently resides and continues to lead the reconstruction of the history of the Triangular Trade.

Atlantic Black Box is a public history project that empowers communities throughout New England to take up the critical work of researching and reckoning with our region's complicity in the slave trade and our extensive involvement in the global economy of enslavement. This grassroots historical recovery movement is powered by citizen historians and guided by a broad coalition of scholars, community leaders, educators, archivists, museum professionals, antiracism activists, and artists.

There is also the thorny question of whether any of our sea captains actually bought and transported Africans for their enslavement in the United States or the West Indies? In the peak year of 1850, there were 50 clipper captains living in Brewster, many of them going to sea on the Triangular Trade route. When they returned home from voyages, they attended the local churches, served in public office, and, with their spouses, created and established the cultural fabric of the town. These families wove the tapestry that enveloped the town with the benefits from enslaving others.

Sally Cabot Gunning, the president of the **Brewster Historical Society,** was generous to spend some time with me explaining the possible connections between our sea captains and the institution of slavery. Sally is an outstanding writer of historical fiction, including her latest book *Monticello*, which tells the Jefferson story from the points of view of his daughter, Martha, and

Sally Hemings, an enslaved woman with whom he fathered several children. Ms. Gunning explained that the Historical Society was working on a new exhibit to open in Spring 2021: **"Were there slaves in Brewster? Yes."** The exhibit will include documentation from wills, bills of sale, diaries, etc. with interpretation by historians. A few examples to be found in the exhibit:

- Brewster became its own town in 1803. Prior to that, Brewster was considered part of Harwich. The "slave census" for Harwich in 1774 included 8 male and 6 female enslaved people.

- In 1755 archives, Thomas Clark of the Brewster gristmill left in his will "little Negro Molly" to his wife.

- In 1760, Benjamin Bangs noted in his diary that his "Negro Oliver" was sold for 39 pounds. Bangs lived across the street from First Parish Brewster, and his home eventually became the parsonage for the Unitarian Church. There is also a bill of sale from Bangs for Sarah for 25 pounds that includes a warranty of sorts stating that if she had tuberculosis, the buyer could recover his money.

- By 1783, the institution of slavery was no longer legal in Massachusetts, and after 1790, no enslaved people were listed on the census. However, many Native Americans and Black people likely remained as indentured servants.

Although Ms. Gunning noted that there is no documented proof of any Brewster captains having direct involvement in the capture and transport of Africans to either the West Indies or the southern states, there were many questions to be answered.

How did we benefit from the institution of slavery in the past and continue to today? Both Sally and Meadow agreed that the entire economy of Cape Cod, and by extension the Northeast, benefited. For example, New England fishermen, including those on Cape Cod, turned away from European markets to make a low-grade salt cod to be shipped to the West Indies to feed those enslaved.

From *History Today:*

"But it was sugar which transformed salt cod from a valuable commodity into an economic sensation. By the late 17th century, much of the Caribbean had been given over to sugar production.... To keep costs down, plantation owners relied increasingly on slaves, brought over from West Africa...plantation owners would have to devote great swathes of their land to crops or animals which they were unwilling to do. Their solution was to give the slaves salt cod instead.

The New England fishermen could hardly believe their luck. Although salt cod was relatively easy to produce, the salting and drying process could go wrong in any one of a number of ways. Since Europeans had become rather particular about the quality of their salt cod, defective produce had previously been thrown away. But plantation owners weren't so picky. Concerned only to feed their slaves cheaply, they would take whatever the New Englanders could supply – provided the price was right. This meant that the New Englanders could turn waste into profit – and a profitable new trade was born."

So the question needed to be asked: if this was happening out of Bristol, RI; New Bedford, MA, New York City, and other Northeast coastal towns, was it happening on Cape Cod as well? And in Brewster?

The answer is yes, and not just with codfish, but our beloved herring as well. Herring was cheap and transported well, so Brewster herring was shipped to the West Indies to feed those enslaved. To underscore the issue of complicity, we ask these questions:

- Who caught the fish? Made the barrels to store the fish?
- Who built and financed the ships? Worked on the ships? Captained the ships?
- In ships' logs there are notes on palm oil, gold dust, ivory, and coffee coming from Africa. What about people?

From looking at the evidence thus far, it seems to me that many Brewster town members of the time were aware of, directly benefited from, and participated in the Triangular Trade.

Ironically, some of these same people, and their descendants, were active in the Unitarian Universalist Church, among other churches, and became ardent abolitionists. I noted that I had connected with the First Parish Brewster group exploring the issue of reparations for their Church's role in the Triangular Trade. The ongoing efforts at First Parish and in communities around the country are an important foundational step toward both reparations and the anti-racism work so desperately needed today.

After this sobering start to our morning, we moved onto the **Cape Cod Rail Trail** to walk through many conservation areas and **Nickerson State Forest**. We noted how conservation plays a role at the local, state, and federal level, in addition to how our federal government had abdicated its role as a protector of the environment and was causing real damage through regressive policies, neglect, and inept management.

At the overlook on **Skaket Beach marsh** we had a conversation about the environment and I shared information from the **Association to Preserve Cape Cod**, the leading environmental group on the Cape. Their website contains many resources for all ages, including tips for creating an eco-friendly landscape. We talked about the rise in harmful blooms of cyanobacteria in Cape ponds due to excessive fertilizers, human and pet waste, and runoff from roadways.

We shared our understandings and hopes regarding climate change, support for wind energy, sustainability, and water protection. We acknowledged that the important work of the environmental and conservation groups on Cape Cod contribute to the health and vitality of both the place itself and its people.

We continued our walk into Orleans Center with a stop at the Hot Chocolate Sparrow for much needed iced coffee. At the picnic tables outside, we debriefed each other on what we had learned thus far, expressing a commitment to explore the ongoing impact of the institution of slavery in this country, and its connections to the history of Cape Cod. After this discussion, all the walkers except for Lauren and myself took their leave for the day.

As Lauren and I continued on to Eastham, we talked about our friends, the Pilgrims, again, since the Mayflower replica had just passed through the Cape Cod Canal on its return to Plymouth after a three-year restoration. I watched the event and had conflicting emotions about the grandeur of the tall ship and its escort of dozens of smaller vessels passing through the canal. The Pilgrims were a persecuted group who left England in search of a better life. Reconciling that fact with how they, in turn, persecuted the Indigenous peoples once here remains a complex history for us to wrestle with.

As we walked near the Orleans' Snow Library, I read a description of Orleans Historical Society's current exhibit, "The Land Called Nawsett":

"Our presentation begins with the region's Native American tribes and their initial encounters-- peaceful and not--with early European explorers and then the Pilgrims on the Mayflower. Next, we recount the expeditions launched from Plymouth to Nauset to find more fertile land to expand and sustain the colony.

Finding that the Outer Cape offered better prospects, at least for some, the Plymouth Colony Court in 1644 gave land grants to each of seven families to settle the area that today includes parts of Orleans and Wellfleet, and all of Eastham. We explore the backgrounds of these founding families, and the imprint their first and second generations left on our history."

I was astounded to read that 7 colonist families were "granted" all this land that was already populated by the native peoples! What did this mean for the Native peoples living there?

Thousands of homes now occupy this same land. For some perspective, we looked at the population of Nauset High School in 2019: 85% White, 5% Black, 4% Hispanic, < 1% Native; 3% one or more races; 23% considered "Low income." What does "low income" mean in a tourist and retiree economy? How are the approximately 10% students of color treated in the school system and in the towns? Does the curriculum only present a narrow, white and western worldview, or does it incorporate other perspectives, use diverse historical sources, and address the effects of colonialism? I recognized that I didn't know enough about the schools on Cape Cod and would seek to learn more about them, not just from administrators and parents, but from students themselves.

We made our way to the new crossing in Eastham that stops traffic on Route 6, a cross-country U.S. Highway otherwise referred to as the Grand Army of the Republic Highway. (I'd never thought about the name before, so I looked it up—the road was named for Union army, navy, and marine veterans of the Civil War.) So, thank you to the MA state highway system for a safe pedestrian crossing on a dangerous road! We continued to note the lack of sidewalks on our travels, and how even those present are not well cared for, with shrubs and weeds blocking the path.

At Fort Hill we took in the breathtaking scenery of the Cape Cod National Seashore: 68 square miles established in 1961 by President Kennedy. The national park includes ponds, woods, and 40 miles of seashore. This forward-looking environmental policy provided generations with protected access to a pristine seashore, a large contrast to the commercial destruction of coastlines as seen in such places as Connecticut, New Jersey, and Florida. No high-rise hotels, casinos, strip malls, etc. have been allowed to degrade its rare natural state. Instead, areas of protected shoreline, marshes, and woodlands as far as the eye can see can still be found.

We made our way to the Skiff Hill overlook. The trail's interpretive signs tell of the Native Americans who settled there, the European explorers including Champlain, and the ecological story of the marsh. **A large boulder used as a sharpening rock by Native Americans** provided a welcome rest stop. A family of four climbed over and sat on the rock, enjoying their time together. I felt uncomfortable, however, and wanted to ask them to move, but questioned if it was my place to bother a mother and her three small children. I felt an urge to protect the rock as a historical artifact of the Native people that should be respected and not treated as a place of play. I also felt frustration that I was at this place of great beauty and historical significance, and I was questioning the parenting of the mother. Over the summer it seemed I was questioning everything, leading to more exploration, learning, and letting go of preconceived judgements.

After leaving Fort Hill, we had a decision to make: it was already noon and almost 90 degrees with high humidity. Both of us were exhausted, and although I wanted to make it to First Encounter Beach where the Pilgrims and Nauset had their first altercation, we both had been to the site several times before. Instead, we continued to the Eastham Windmill on Rt 6 and crossed over to Salt Pond Visitor Center for the end of our day.

We sat overlooking the pond and recounted the day and our past six weeks of walks across Cape Cod. Lauren and I had developed a rhythm to our walks each week, and supported each other as we explored the stories hidden all around us. We sat in silent meditation giving thanks for another day in deep communion with other walkers, the stories of history, and the sacred places we had travelled. I then walked down to the Salt Pond and dove in to refresh myself. I would sit for two hours in the shade by the pond reflecting on the Camino Way experience of the summer—both the inner and outer journey that was occurring. All parts of me were opening, expanding, growing, questioning. And through the interaction with others along the way, I was moving in new directions for my life. I didn't know exactly where all of this was leading me, but I was engaging with both history and current issues in ways that would engender new directions, and for that I was extremely grateful.

Resources:
"A History of Salt Cod", History Today
https://www.historytoday.com/archive/historians-cookbook/history-salt-cod
Association to Preserve Cape Cod
https://apcc.org/
The Atlantic Black Box Project
https://atlanticblackbox.com/Brewster Historical Society
Brewster Historical Society
https://www.brewsterhistoricalsociety.org/
Cape Cod National Seashore
https://www.nps.gov/caco/index.htm
Complicity: How the North Promoted, Prolonged, and Profited from Slavery
by Anne Farrow, Joel Lang, and Jenifer Frank
First Parish Brewster Unitarian Universalist's work on reparations
https://atlanticblackbox.com/2021/03/09/first-parish-brewster-uu-mass-reparations/
Nickerson State Park
https://www.mass.gov/locations/nickerson-state-park
Orleans Historical Society
https://www.orleanshistoricalsociety.org/
Rainbow Peace Flag Project
https://commonstreet.org/rainbow-peace-flag-project/
"What Was the Triangle Trade?", Thought Co.
https://www.thoughtco.com/triangle-trade-104592

Create Your Own Walk with Friends and Family

Several options exist for a shorter version of this walk that would provide a focus on either the environment or the history of the Cape economy and its connections to the institution of slavery.

Option 1: Park behind First Parish Brewster Unitarian church and start in the graveyard, exploring the headstones for clues about the sea captains and their families. Take in several of the large inns of Brewster (Captain Freeman, Candleberry, Old Manse, etc.) on your walk and read stories on their websites about their historical significance. Begin your walk up Rt 6A, past the Brewster General Store, perhaps pausing there to explore their selection of historical artifacts and books. Continue past the Brewster Ladies' Library, and if open, view their historical photographs and original front rooms. The library was constructed in the late 1800s by the town with the support of a dedicated group of women readers. Pass the old Brewster Town Hall and the Veterans Memorial. Continue past the Latham Center and the former Fire Museum. Take a right on Swamp Rd, one of the original roads in Brewster, and follow it down to Lower Rd. Cross over to the Brewster Cemetery and seek out the headstones of the sea captains and their families. Make the connections of where they travelled to and died—the southern states, the Caribbean, Africa, etc. Continue east on Lower Rd past the Eddy Sisters homes and the Community Gardens. Take the half-mile loop into the woods at the Community Gardens, and learn about the conservation efforts there. Follow Lower Rd to the Captain Cobb House and the Brewster Historical Society, and if open, spend an hour exploring their wonderful exhibits and grounds. Return to the Brewster General Store for refreshments, including ice cream! – 2-3 miles, depending on loops taken

Option 2: Focus on the environment by spending the day in Nickerson State Park, with miles of walking and biking trails, ranger-led programs, fishing and swimming ponds, and opportunities to learn about conservation and nature. Take a walk or bike ride from Nickerson across 6A down Crosby Ln to view the Crosby mansion and the expanse of bay beach there. – Length: as long as you'd like to make it!

Option 3: Park at Fort Hill lookout or the lower parking lot and walk the trails around the perimeter of the property, from the top of the hill with vistas to Coast Guard and Nauset Beaches, to the marsh and the birds fishing along the shore. Walk by the Captain Penniman House and read the interpretive signs explaining the home and the lands. Continue into the swamp area and forest on the weather-proof walking path and take the extension over to Hemenway Landing to see the ocean inlet, the boaters, and walk along the shore. Read the stories about the Nauset tribe and the European explorers in this area, and touch the sharpening rock to feel the work of the Natives in its grooves. This hike is outstanding for its views, nature, and history, and is suitable for all ages. – 1-3 miles, depending on route taken

Walk 7
Cultural Kaleidoscope – The Arts

> *"Black is the beauty*
> *Of the night forever and ever*
> *Black is what brings light"*
>
> -Nikkiesha McLeod, "BLACK"

August 19, 2020

Towns: Wellfleet, Truro

Route: Begin at the parking lot of the Cape Cod Rail Trail on Lecount Hollow Rd. Follow Lecount Hollow to Ocean View Dr, to turn left on Cahoon Hollow Rd. Follow it to Rt 6 and cross to follow north a few yards and turn left onto Main St. Follow Main St to Wellfleet Preservation Hall for a break. Continue on Main St, bearing right onto West Main and continuing right onto Pole Dike Rd. Follow Pole Dike until turning left onto Bound Brook Island Rd, then bear right at the next fork onto Pamet Point Rd. Turn left on Old County Rd and follow until it turns into Depot Rd, then turn left on Truro Center Rd to end at Pamet River Park. – 12 miles (with hills!)

Sites:
- Wellfleet Preservation Hall
- Cape Cod National Seashore
- Billingsgate Island
- Truro Center for the Arts at Castle Hill
- Truro Historical Society

Issues Explored:
- Black, Indigenous and People of Color in the arts
- The Pilgrims, again
- History of enslaved peoples in Truro

This week, 9 others joined me for the beginning of the walk on Lecount Hollow Rd in Wellfleet to the center of town via Ocean View Dr. Several of the walkers were from Springfield, MA, and had attended Cathedral High School with me or my sister. Kathy, Kate, Lucy, and Candace joined for the first time; Lauren joined us for her 7th walk; and other returners included my sister Marie, Wilderness, Saffron, and Licia. I was blessed to have these women join in the walk, and more importantly, in the conversation and learning experience.

For this walk, we focused on Black, Indigenous, and People of Color in the arts, and on current issues in the United States related to race. We began with introductions and set an intention for our participation in the walk. We honored the Native people and lands we would walk, being reminded that all of Cape Cod once belonged to the Wampanoag nation. I'd prepared the container for this week's journey with some research and historical information for the route we'd travel. Several other participants contributed inspirations from writers, poets, visual artists, and musicians—all people of color. We first discussed the selection of Kamala Harris to run for Vice President of the United States, the first Black and Indian woman to do so. We also highlighted the outstanding speech delivered by Michelle Obama at the Democratic Convention that week. Regardless of party, we were excited to see these women shine in our political process.

To begin our experience, I shared a powerful poem by my sister-in-law's sister, Nikkie, a Trinidadian-born poet and musician from New York City. Since the pandemic began, our family had held several Friday evening Zoom calls where Nikkie shared her poetry and music with us. Looking back, one of the positives of the pandemic year would be the many Zoom sessions with family and friends to maintain and strengthen connections.

BLACK
by Nikkiesha McLeod

We're at the same juncture where Black people are met with the same struggle, one which seems to never end. We're still fighting for our lives to matter. We still can't breathe as the knees of oppression bends into our necks, killing us. We've peacefully marched, we've walked with our anger boiling beneath our rich and beautiful skin, but yet this ugly history of us being beaten down, being hosed down still continues today. A reflection of us standing up against the fences, the faces of an established denial of my place in the world, where I dream as much as you do. I wish to sing my troubles. But it is the same tune. What else is there for us to say out loud, write down and shout, We shall overcome...Should I tell the next generation it's up to them now, to carry this anger, this despair, this anxiety of living outside, while I can't even escape it myself? My life is ordinary like the songs of any bird-call voicing an incandescent sound, but because of the hatred of my existence I am martyred for my race, for my color: Black!

Black is the beauty
of the night forever and ever
Black is what brings light.

I also mentioned that one of Nikkie's musical pieces can be heard at:
https://share.icloud.com/photos/0jvkc_ZqVldElwEOSINOac4xg

I shared with the group that I had returned to the **Atwood Museum** exhibit (from Walk 5) that focused on the Wampanoag and Mayflower stories—where they connected and the impact they had on each other. The Atwood also had a new exhibit on World War II, and I'd noticed a Black woman in a photo as "Rosie the Riveter," something I had never seen before. There was another photo of a "sugar rationing" line that included white boys, and black and white women. I wondered if the photo was taken in the North because the line was integrated. It is rare to see images of Black people on the walls of Cape Cod museums, so I had sought out the curator of the exhibit nearby and thanked him.

I made the group aware of a special exhibit incorporating the Wampanoag story at the Wellfleet Historical Society and Museum: "**Before 1620: Who Was Here?**" This provided an option for those who left the walk mid-day in Wellfleet. Through numerous artifacts, the exhibit acknowledged the Native presence back to 10,000 BCE and questioned stereotypes, examining the past through some unusual lenses. We spoke of the Pilgrims' landing in Provincetown and Truro, searching for drinking water in the Pilgrim Spring area, coming ashore at Corn Hill to steal Nauset corn, and skirmishing with the Nauset at First Encounter Beach in Eastham. No, Plymouth Rock was NOT the first place the Pilgrims stepped foot in America!

We ventured down Lecount Hollow Rd, with small groups of 3-4 people sharing their life stories and why they were walking that day. Some of these women had known each other for 40-50 years, and were exploring the history and culture of People of Color on Cape Cod in a new and different way. Everyone welcomed conversation and the group gelled quickly. We stopped for our first break at White Crest Beach on the Atlantic shore in Wellfleet, and took in the vast ocean in front of us while contemplating the inner thoughts of a poet of color. Wilderness had shared a deeply impactful poem by Lucille Clifton, an American poet, writer, and educator from Buffalo, New York. From 1974 to 1985 she served as the Poet Laureate of Maryland. Clifton became the first author to have two books of poetry named finalists for one year's Pulitzer Prize. "A prolific and widely respected poet, Clifton's work emphasizes endurance and strength through adversity, focusing particularly on African-American experience and family life."

We continued walking with a sense of heaviness about the lives lost to systemic racism, the violence that continued to play out on a regular basis, like a dripping faucet, across the country over the summer. Violence, we all agreed, must stop. Systems, we all agreed, needed to change.

At the Beachcomber, a popular hangout perched on a dune cliff where a boisterous crowd is normally found, an eerie quiet greeted us on the bluff. Suspended above the great ocean, we listened intently as Kate shared with her brilliant voice excerpts from *The Woman Who Fell from the Sky* by U.S. Poet Laureate Joy Harjo. Harjo, an internationally renowned performer and writer of the Muscogee (Creek) Nation, draws on storytelling and histories, as well as feminist and social justice poetic traditions.

She incorporates indigenous myths, symbols, and values into her writing, and her poetry connects deeply with landscapes—the Southwest, Southeast, Alaska, and Hawaii. According to her bio on the Poetry Foundation, she once commented,

"I feel strongly that I have a responsibility to all the sources that I am: to all past and future ancestors, to my home country, to all places that I touch down on and that are myself, to all voices, all women, all of my tribe, all people, all earth, and beyond that to all beginnings and endings. In a strange kind of sense [writing] frees me to believe in myself, to be able to speak, to have voice, because I have to; it is my survival."

At our next stop at Great Pond, Saffron shared a few visual artists she'd enjoyed exploring in preparation for the walk. She described the work of each artist and showed them on her phone. With good spritzes of hand sanitizer, we passed the phone to each person drawn into to images. The two artists she was inspired by were:

• **Shirin Neshat**: an Iranian visual artist who lives in New York City. Her artwork centers on the contrasts between Islam and the West, femininity and masculinity, public life and private life, antiquity and modernity. Her work of Arabic writing covering women's faces and hands was striking to behold.

• **Aaqil Ka**: a scenic artist for film and television based in Brooklyn, NY, inspired by nature, culture, technology, and social issues.

Shirin Neshat, Identified, 1995 Photo: Cynthia Preston, https://storyboard.cmoa.org/2015/06/how-shirin-neshats-identified-series-speaks-through-its-silence/

We remarked on how art is such a powerful tool to learn about and connect with cultures other than our own. Several of our walks were enriched through Saffron's participation. As a teenager attending Nauset High, she embodies a depth of knowledge and understanding that touched us deeply.

Licia, walking with us for the third time, shared the inspiration she'd found in Frida Kahlo's self-portraits, with their pain and passion, and bold, vibrant colors. Kahlo is a prominent figure in both the art and feminist worlds, celebrated for the inspiration and representation of her Mexican heritage and culture found in her work, as well as her depiction of the female experience and form.

Aaqil Ka, *Carmen de Lavallade* (2012) Mixed Media on canvas
https://www.blkcatbone.com/carmen

We continued on to Wellfleet Center, crossing Route 6 at the traffic light— a very dangerous undertaking. One thing we noticed in each town along our journey was a lack of attention to pedestrian safety and access to our Cape Cod road system. In many places there were no sidewalks, forcing us to use extreme caution in unsafe conditions. In others, the sidewalks were so overgrown and in such poor condition that walking was treacherous. I also observed many drivers going too fast on all roadways, and barely giving way for pedestrians. I will consider my own actions as a driver a bit differently having done these walks all summer.

We rested and enjoyed a conversation in a circle in the garden behind Wellfleet Preservation Hall. As several in our group planned to finish their walk there, I asked everyone to share something they would take away from the day's experience. Many people were visibly moved as they shared:

- "I'm going to think about the ugly history referenced in the poem—what are our monuments?"
- "I was aware of my privilege to walk freely, with the walk reminding me of being at Standing Rock three years ago, and returning to the Cape with more awareness that all Land in the U.S. was homeland of the Indigenous people."
- "I'm honored to be with people looking at our history, sharing stories: What does celebrating 400 mean?"
- "I was so glad to see the visual arts today, remember Frida Kahlo, and acknowledge a friend I lost recently by sharing a poem on her land with everyone."
- "I was reminded about the suffrage movement, how that is tainted too with the story of whiteness. In order to celebrate the suffragettes, we have to recognize that Black women were excluded."
- "Sharing the poems today, listening to the readings and perspectives was powerful. Just walking with all of you."

Kate then reminded us we saw a heron that day, and quoted Mary Oliver's poem, "**Heron Rises from the Dark, Summer Pond**," from memory, inspiring us to explore more of Oliver's lovely poetry about nature on Cape Cod.

Kate, Lauren, and I marched on another five miles in the August heat along the backroads of Wellfleet, going up and down some serious hills. At a rest stop in the shade atop a hill by a cemetery, I shared the image and words of a nearby memorial site to encourage us to return for more exploration.

HERE LIES
AN INDIAN WOMAN
A
WAMPANOAG
WHOSE FAMILY AND TRIBE
GAVE OF THEMSELVES
AND THEIR LAND
THAT THIS GREAT NATION
MIGHT BE BORN AND GROW

REINTERRED HERE MAY 30, 1976
WAMPANOAG TRIBAL COUNCIL
WELLFLEET HISTORICAL SOCIETY

Photo by J.W. Ocker
https://www.oddthingsiveseen.com/2020/09/
graves-and-gravestones-of-cape-cod-part.html

The memorial with the "gifts of respect" is positioned flat upon the ground, adjacent to the National Seashore parking lot at the entrance to Great Island.

We looked at the fascinating story of Billingsgate Island, not far from where we were resting. All three of us had been on or near Billingsgate before, but knew little of its history. From *Cape Cod Life*:

> "Looking out over the horizon of Wellfleet Harbor evokes a feeling of nostalgia. One feels a sense of history, a stillness in time. And just over a century ago, a gleaming light emanating from Billingsgate Island off the coast represented an efficient fishing village full of hardworking families and boaters.... Today, all that remains of Billingsgate Island is an occasional sandbar a few miles off Wellfleet's Jeremy Point.... When the Pilgrims arrived in the region in 1620, the town of Billingsgate (which at the time included Eastham and Wellfleet—and the 60-acre island) was home to the Punonakanit people—members of the Wampanoag Federation.... According to *A History Of Billingsgate* by Durand Echeverria, the Native Americans and the Europeans who settled in the Billingsgate community coexisted peacefully until smallpox eventually shrunk the Billingsgate Punonakanit population to just 11 in 1694. Originally settled by the Europeans as a fishing village, the island was most likely named after the famous Billingsgate fishing market of London."

This account led to the obvious questions: Who "originally settled" the land? Who brought the smallpox that practically wiped out the Punonakanit population? We were reminded to read historical accounts carefully, and determine the perspective and intent of the writer.

I shared the below press release with the walkers to highlight the current issues of federal recognition that continue to face the Wampanoag Nation today. On May 5, 2020, the Barnstable County Human Rights Advisory Commission issued this statement:

BARNSTABLE COUNTY HUMAN RIGHTS ADVISORY COMMISSION SUPPORTS THE MASHPEE WAMPANOAG TRIBE

The Barnstable County Human Rights Advisory Commission (HRAC) supports Mashpee Wampanoag Tribe in action against Department of Interior.

The Human Rights Advisory Commission of Barnstable County, out of respect for the Mashpee Wampanoag Tribe and the long, traumatic history they endured, express our extreme displeasure with the Department of Interior's recent decision denying the Tribe's right to hold land in trust.

At a time when we are collectively sharing significant challenges and together experiencing a period of tremendous hardship, the HRAC hopes that the Department focuses on the immense value of the Tribe and work to ensure a path of cooperation and respect.

2020 is the year that we commemorate the 400th anniversary of the Mayflower voyage and the founding of Plymouth Colony. This history cannot be told without honoring the immense contribution of the Wampanoag people that are still among us. Thus, we urge the Department to initiate a complete review of the denial and engage in the process of reconsideration that accounts for the full history of this great Tribe. Fairness dictates no other course of action.

We three walkers fell into easy silences and our own thoughts as we made our way for the last few miles, passing by farms, modern homes, the marsh at sea level, and forested hills with large boulders. We encouraged each other in the humidity to seek whatever shade we could along the road. We spoke of concerts attended over the past few summers at the Payomet Performing Arts Center, a non-profit organization dedicated to producing exciting performing arts rooted in strong social values. During this final hour we saw only a few bicyclists and enjoyed the quiet solitude.

Kate reminded us as we passed by the Truro Center for the Arts at Castle Hill that she worked there part-time, and that the staff had developed a statement to support eradicating racism in the arts. We reflected on this statement, similar to many others across all industries that summer, and its commitment to being part of the change.

From the Board and Staff of the Truro Center for the Arts

To Our Valued Community:

George Floyd was murdered more than a month ago and it feels like the world has shifted seismically since then, finally acknowledging the persistence of the cruel racial and economic disparities that blight our country. The Truro Center for the Arts at Castle Hill counts inclusivity as a core value but we have not achieved the diversity to which we aspire. Our Board and Staff welcome this moment of historical change and the opportunity it presents to examine ourselves and make the changes necessary to create an arts community that welcomes, serves and nurtures Black, Asian, LatinX and all Indigenous artists.

We strive to create an environment that encourages artists of all types and experiences, but we clearly still have far to go. We will begin by immediately establishing a committee of board members, staff and faculty and giving them a charge to examine our practices to identify instances of implicit bias and ways in which we operate that may discourage broader participation. They will recommend changes needed to remove obstacles and things we must do proactively to extend our hand to engage actively with under-represented communities. We will examine our leadership, our partnerships and our programs to find ways to do better. We aim to do this as soon as we possibly can.

We stand in support of those who have dedicated themselves to the struggle for racial and economic justice. We commit to doing our part.

I also shared information from the Truro Historical Society, and although we didn't walk by there that day, we agreed to return to see the exhibit described below. Most people today can't imagine that enslaved people lived in Truro. Also provided below is a sample "land acknowledgement" that mirrored what we used at the beginning of each of our walks.

Our Support for Racial Justice

The Truro Historical Society (THS) supports the peaceful Black Lives Matter movement for racial justice that is taking place in the United States and around the world. 'Liberty and justice for all' means justice for Black and Indigenous populations, and for all people of color.

Museums and archives are not neutral spaces. Because we interpret history, we have the responsibility of presenting the past as fully and accurately as possible, including painful and uncomfortable aspects. The past feeds into the present, and when a community actively engages with its past, it can use its understanding to make a better society.

Truro was founded on land that had been inhabited by Native People for thousands of years, but these people were displaced by English settlers. There were enslaved people and indentured laborers enduring near-slavery conditions in Truro. In 1754, the town's first minister, Reverend John Avery, bequeathed to his children three African-American enslaved men and 'my Indian Girl Sarah.'

After reflecting on the 'settler privilege' that most of us enjoy, the THS decided in late 2019 to mark the 400th anniversary of the Pilgrims' arrival with a decolonial exhibition celebrating Truro's first inhabitants, the Wampanoag Nation, from its origins to today. During the postponement caused by the coronavirus, the THS will continue to consult with Indigenous scholars and community members. We will increase our commitment to diversity and inclusion. As a token of our commitment, the THS wishes to share the Land Acknowledgment we have prepared in consultation with members of the Wampanoag Nation. This statement will stand at the entrance to the Highland House Museum's permanent exhibition about the Paomet and the Wampanoag peoples.

Land Acknowledgment
The Highland House Museum stands on the traditional homeland of the Paomet Tribe, members of the Wampanoag Nation, who have inhabited Cape Cod for more than 12,000 years and who knew this part of Truro as Tashmuit. The Truro Historical Society acknowledges the displacement, suffering, and forced assimilation of the Wampanoag and other Native Peoples caused by European contact and colonization. We honor the struggles of the Wampanoag, People of the First Light, and support their resilience, and we ask museum visitors to reflect on our shared responsibility to maintain social justice.

At the end of our hike at the Pamet River Park in Truro, Kate shared one last poem from Joy Harjo that provided the "dessert" for our long day of walking. We sat at a picnic table, with tears welling in our eyes as we reflected on the poignancy of being at a table, and the messages found in Harjo's stunning poem:

Perhaps the World Ends Here
by Joy Harjo

The world begins at a kitchen table. No matter what, we must eat to live.

The gifts of earth are brought and prepared, set on the table. So it has been since creation, and it will go on.

We chase chickens or dogs away from it. Babies teethe at the corners. They scrape their knees under it.

It is here that children are given instructions on what it means to be human. We make men at it, we make women.

At this table we gossip, recall enemies and the ghosts of lovers.

Our dreams drink coffee with us as they put their arms around our children. They laugh with us at our poor falling-down selves and as we put ourselves back together once again at the table.

This table has been a house in the rain, an umbrella in the sun.

Wars have begun and ended at this table. It is a place to hide in the shadow of terror. A place to celebrate the terrible victory.

We have given birth on this table, and have prepared our parents for burial here.

At this table we sing with joy, with sorrow. We pray of suffering and remorse. We give thanks.

Perhaps the world will end at the kitchen table, while we are laughing and crying, eating of the last sweet bite.

Resources:

Barnstable County Human Rights Advisory Commission
https://www.barnstablecountyhrac.org/
Cape Cod National Seashore
https://www.nps.gov/caco/index.htm
"Heron Rises from the Dark, Summer Pond"
by Mary Oliver
http://dallasegrets.org/?page_id=120
Joy Harjo, U.S. Poet Laureate
https://www.joyharjo.com/
Lucille Clifton
https://www.poetryfoundation.org/poets/lucille-clifton
Payomet Performing Arts Center
https://payomet.org/
"Perhaps the World Ends Here", from *The Woman Who Fell From the Sky* by
Joy Harjo
https://www.poetryfoundation.org/poems/49622/perhaps-the-world-ends-
here
"There's history — and mystery — beneath the waters off Wellfleet"
by Liam Russo, *Cape Cod Life*, 2015
https://capecodlife.com/billingsgate-island-wellfleet/
Truro Center for the Arts at Castle Hill
https://www.castlehill.org/
Truro Historical Society
https://trurohistoricalsociety.org/
Wellfleet Historical Society & Museum
http://www.wellfleethistoricalsociety.org/
Wellfleet Preservation Hall
https://www.wellfleetpreservationhall.org/

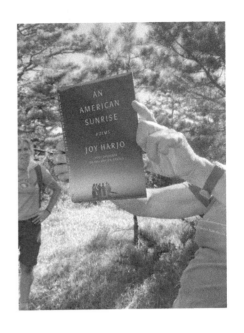

Create Your Own Walk with Friends and Family

For a walk in the town of Wellfleet, park in the Main St lot in the center of town and cross the street to Preservation Hall. Begin in their garden with a recognition of the lands you will be walking and an intention to be open to the stories of all people who cross your path. Walk up Main St towards Holbrook Ave and turn left, passing by historical homes for 0.7 miles to the harbor. Take in the oyster beds offshore and, if it's a nice day, consider walking for 0.5 miles on Mayo Beach thinking about the Wampanoag peoples that lived and fished nearby, and the present-day oyster farmers. Return to town via Commercial St, again noting the art galleries representing various styles and traditions. Take a left on Bank St, then right onto Main to visit the Wellfleet Historical Society & Museum. For a longer walk on quiet roads (no sidewalk), continue to the left on School St, left on Mill Hill Rd, and left on Ryder Ct to return back to Main St.

Other walks in Wellfleet include the Marconi Wireless Station site (1-2 miles) or the Great Island Trail (4-8 miles). Both are found on the Cape Cod National Seashore website.

Walk 8
Land's End: Pilgrims, Poets, and Provincetown

> *"Driving over the hill from Truro into Provincetown, I have always been struck by the beauty of shimmering water on both sides of the road, the Truro cottages ticking by uniformly at the water's edge. Taking the time to walk this path of beauty allowed for a space of reverence, both individual and communal, in which to process the insightful questions Peggy posed about the town, its people, its stories, and its legacy."*
>
> -Chloe Heidepriem, *AmeriCorps VISTA at Helping Our Women*

August 26, 2020

Towns: Truro, Provincetown

Route: From Truro Public Library, turn right onto Shore Rd/Route 6A and follow into Provincetown. Turn right on Conwell St, cross Rt 6 onto Race Point Rd and turn into the Beech Forest parking lot. Pick up the Province Lands Bike Trail on the left to Herring Cove Beach, continue on Province Lands Rd to Pilgrim's First Landing Park, then follow Commercial St to Provincetown Town Hall, Portuguese Square, and Bas Relief Park. – 12 miles

Sites:
- Truro Public Library
- Helping Our Women
- Cape Cod National Seashore
- Pilgrim's First Landing Park
- Pilgrim Monument and Provincetown Museum
- Provincetown Veterans Memorial & AIDS Memorial

Issues Explored:
- The Pilgrim Story revisited from the Nauset perspective
- Resources in a pandemic
- LGBQT+ issues
- Provincetown Tennessee Williams Theater Festival's 2020 theme of Censorship
- Land's End: Provincetown Artist Colony
- Closing Circle for the Cape Cod Camino Way

We gathered at the Truro Public Library to begin the last walk of our 2020 summer on the Cape Cod Camino Way. Chloe Heidepriem, the Volunteer Resource Developer at Provincetown's **Helping Our Women**, Bob Ross, a psychologist and local artist, and Lauren, my reliable weekly walker, joined me that morning in honoring the Native lands we would pass over, and setting our intentions for the day. I wanted to be fully present for this last walk, taking in all that was around me and exploring what that summer of walking had meant to me personally. I couldn't believe we had started just two months earlier at the Canal, had made our way through all the towns on the Cape, and were embarking on our last miles to "Land's End."

I explained to the walkers in the Library parking lot that for thousands of years North Truro, and Cape Cod in general, was home to the Nauset and Paomet (Pamet), distinct tribes from the Wampanoag people. Nanepashemet, a Wampanoag member of the late 20th century (1954-1995), described of the Wampanoag philosophy regarding their relationship with the land:

"We have lived with this land for thousands of generations- fishing in the waters, planting and harvesting crops, hunting the four-legged and winged beings and giving respect and thanks for each and every thing taken for our use."

I started our walk with a recognition of the Nauset and Wampanoag's experience of the Pilgrims' arrival 400 years ago. The echoes of that significant event, which changed the history of this country, had somehow been with us every week over the summer of 2020. It had manifested most as the taught version of the *Mayflower* voyage: the Pilgrims were persecuted in England, sailed to America, landed at Plymouth Rock, and were welcomed by the "Indians." But a more accurate version would read like this:

On November 21, 1620, the *Mayflower*, with 132 people aboard, landed in what is now known as Provincetown Harbor. Soon after their arrival, an exploratory party led by Myles Standish and William Bradford explored present-day Truro. They discovered fresh water at Pilgrim Spring and spent the night by Pilgrim Pond. On November 26, they came upon a Nauset stash of corn that they stole to use as seed for planting, worried that their European grains would not grow in new world soil. This discovery was made on what is now known as Corn Hill. On December 16, the Pilgrims traveled to Eastham, where they confronted members of the Nauset tribe in the event now known as "First Encounter." Several days later, the *Mayflower* set sail for mainland more suitable for settling, and landed at Patuxet, an abandoned Wampanoag village, on December 26, 1620, to found Plymouth Colony. They had spent just over one month anchored in Provincetown Harbor.

Pilgrim Pond Park in Truro marks the location where that first Pilgrim expedition party spent their second night in the new world, and this is recognized by a plaque citing the event and the names of the Pilgrims. The plaque reads:

> Sixteen Pilgrims
> Led By
> Myles Standish, William Bradford,
> Stephen Hawkins and Edward Tilley
> Encamped on the shore of this pond
> for their second night on American Soil
> November 16, 1620
> Old Style
> Drank their first New England Water
> three miles northeast from here at the
> PILGRIM SPRING
> Found the precious Indian Corn two
> miles southwest from here at
>
> CORN HILL
>
> Provincetown Tercentenary Commission

Of course, what is missing on this plaque was a recognition that the corn was part of a Nauset burial ground, and the Pilgrims had disturbed a sacred place, stolen the corn, and disrupted the site. Actually, the Pilgrims disrupted several burial sites. A more accurate understanding of the interaction between the people already here and the newly arrived Pilgrims was in order that morning, so I shared this alternative perspective:

The people who we now term "Pilgrims" were Separatists who left England, lived in the Netherlands for about 15 years, and then wanted to live free from religious persecution. With sponsorship from several prominent merchants, the *Mayflower* sailed for the "new world" in 1620. On board were the Separatists; the crew, whose knowledge of North America was very limited; and the Strangers, non-Separatist tradesmen, families, indentured servants, and Merchant Adventurers — the investors in this new "colony."

They were delayed six weeks from crossing, leaving much later in the fall season than planned, and took 66 days to cross from Plymouth, England to Cape Cod. They were short on water, lacked any fresh vegetables, and, due to Atlantic storms and rough seas, missed their original destination of the Hudson River, considered the northern edge of the Virginia Colony at the time. They got caught up off the coast of Chatham in Pollock Rip Shoal, and made the fateful decision to heave to and travel up the coast past what is now Eastham, Wellfleet, and Truro to round the hook to find "Milford Haven" harbor, as it had been named a few years earlier by English explorers.

The Separatists were thrilled to finally have the chance to worship freely. The Merchant Adventurers had a sense of relief and optimism for future financial gain and prosperity. The crew was frustrated they were not where they were supposed to be. The rest of the "Strangers" just wanted to get off the boat.

With uncertainty and apprehension at being in a new land different than their Virginia Company charter, and thus facing dissent and defiance from Strangers who felt they were outside government rule, the Pilgrims created the **Mayflower Compact** to establish a temporary set of laws for ruling themselves in their new colony.

To put this story into today's immigration climate and context: the Mayflower passengers were, in fact, illegal immigrants representing a racial minority on their new continent. They had no right to "settle" a land for which they had no contract. Furthermore, such contracts were granted by a nation that had no right to "colonize." The concept of land ownership was antithetical to the Nauset and Wampanoag people already living here. Plus, the "majority agreement" of the Compact wasn't a true majority, as all the women and some indentured servants weren't given a vote.

Additionally, the *Mayflower* Compact, which would influence future foundational documents of the United States, was not the first example of democracy in the "new world." The Algonquins in present-day New York state had a flourishing democratic confederacy which would also later influence some of the framers of the Constitution.

> **To continue a more accurate recounting of events:** over the course of late November and early December, 1620, the Pilgrims would wander through Truro on both sides of the coast and disturb three more burial grounds. They found seasonal **wetu** by the coast indicating the Nauset had moved inland. They took several articles belonging to the Nauset, including the best pot to cook with. On December 8, some Pilgrim men exploring in a shallop off now-Eastham decided to spend the night on land. In the morning they were attacked by the Nauset, and responded with muskets. They got in their boat and sailed down past present-day Brewster and Dennis, with a snowstorm preventing them from seeing Sandy Neck or Barnstable Harbor. Otherwise, it is highly probable they would have settled there for its fresh water, deep harbor, herring runs, and cleared land.

> On December 25, 1620, the Mayflower left for the spot chosen for their new settlement, Patuxet, a former Wampanoag village that had been abandoned a few years earlier because of a devastating plague, likely introduced by Europeans, that swept through the region.

I reminded our walkers of how the Plymouth Colony gave descendants of Mayflower passengers, including 7 families, all of Eastham and part of Orleans to settle. On our Barnstable walk in July, we had met Mercy Otis Warren, another descendent of a Mayflower passenger. She was a writer, historian, poet, and activist, and had contributed to the writing of the Bill of Rights. She was another reminder that the history of Cape Cod and our region is directly connected to the actions of the Mayflower and other European settlers.

I asked the walkers to consider the perspective of the Cape's Indigenous peoples: white settlers arriving to colonize their lands, take their crops, disturb their graves, and spread their foreign ways—religious, political, cultural. I noted that the former Plimoth Plantation had recently changed their name to **Plimoth Patuxet Museums** to recognize the importance of the site's original name and the 50 years of cooperation of the nearby Wampanoag with the new settlement. Many of the Pilgrims were of a persecuted group who had left England in search of a better life. Reconciling that fact with how they treated the Indigenous peoples here remains an open question that connects to the current questions surrounding the status of the Wampanoag tribe, federal recognition issues, reparations for past injustices, and many other complicated issues.

I mentioned that I had noticed some historical inaccuracies in the seal of the town of Truro, which is also featured on the service patch of the Truro Police Department. The town of Truro, Massachusetts, was incorporated in 1709 after being settled nine years earlier by British colonists from the nearby town of Eastham. In the center of the seal, a Nauset man in a headdress, presumably meant to represent a "chief," is shown next to a stalk of corn, the food source which ensured the pilgrims' survival during their first years. His community is represented by two teepees on the right, while the *Mayflower* is shown at sea on the left.

Yet, the Nauset did not dress that way, including the headdress, they did not live in teepees or on the shore, and the stalk of corn represents something that was stolen from them by the Pilgrims. Finally, it appears that the Nauset man depicted was greeting the ship, when there is no record of that actually occurring.

Our second area of focus for the day was the enslavement of Black and Indigenous people in Truro, and generally on Cape Cod. I shared some information from Walk 6 where we focused on the issue of the sea captains and the Triangular Trade of sugar, rum, and enslaved people.

As Henry C. Kittredge observed in *Cape Cod: Its People and Their History*, "slaves were common in all parts of the old colony, and if there were fewer on the Cape then elsewhere, it was only because there were fewer rich men or extensive land owners."

The Cape's first people in bondage were Native Americans. One example: in 1678 three Wampanoag broke into the Sandwich home of Zachariah Allen, prompting the court to decree them lifelong indentured servants to the Allens, with no hope of earning their freedom. Subsequent to King Philip's war, many Native Americans were sold into bondage.

By the 18th century, most of the Cape's slaves were of African descent, and were recorded in many town censuses, wills, bills of sale, etc. Several local place names are inspired by enslaved peoples. Shebnah Rich's book, *Truro Cape Cod, Or, Land Marks and Sea Marks*, mentions a boy named Hector, who at 3 years of age in 1725 was sold to Benjamin Collins. Hector served the Paynes throughout his life and was buried in an unmarked grave, but a section of Truro is still known as "Hector's Stubble." Also found in the area of South Pamet Rd is "Hector's Bridge," "Hector's Nook," and "Old Hector." Another of Payne's enslaved men, Pomp, committed suicide, though his name still lives on in Truro's "Pomp's Lot."

Cape Codders also had a complicated history with abolition. During an 1848 anti-slavery convention in Harwich, 2,000 people stormed the meeting and ran the abolitionists out of town. More liberal Cape residents, however, participated in the Underground Railroad by hiding runaways in their homes, including in four documented places in Provincetown. After the Fugitive Slave Law of 1850 was passed, demanding the return of runaways to their masters, more Northerners refused to comply and opposition to the enslavement of other humans grew stronger. On Sept. 22, 1860, the Cape Cod Anti-Slavery Convention assembled in Harwich Exchange Hall insisted upon "Immediate and Unconditional Abolition." The Cape and region's complicated history with the enslavement of people of color and abolitionism continues today with efforts to promote reparations and anti-racist work in our communities.

Provincetown was one of the largest whaling ports in the United States after New Bedford and Nantucket, which led the way in the industry. You can still see the difference in wealth on Nantucket and in New Bedford, found in the size of the homes and their furnishings. We also acknowledged the salt cod industry as the backbone of Provincetown's prosperity. Provincetown was a leading producer of the main food supply, dried cod, for those enslaved on the sugar plantations in the West Indies. Several blocks of Commercial Street were lined with cod hung up to dry, with very little quality control regulating its safety for consumption.

After this long introduction of the day's topics in the parking lot of the Truro Public Library, we began our walk along several miles of Route 6A from Truro into Provincetown. We were glad to have a local artist with us, and Bob shared several interesting facts about Truro's history and the local housing situation. He pointed out the affordable housing on Shore Rd and the rentals along the bus route where many of the people who work in the tourism industry live, including many people of color. I knew that many people from the Caribbean worked in the tourism industry in Provincetown and across the Cape, but I didn't expect to find such a large number living in Truro. I always thought of Truro as an "exclusive" community. Once again, my assumptions were proven incorrect.

As we walked along Shore Rd, we remarked how different this part of 6A was from the historic districts we walked in Yarmouth Port and Dennis. There were no sidewalks, no beautiful inns and restaurants, no stately homes. Yes, there were some well-off neighborhoods filled with expensive homes along 6A in Truro, but we mostly saw cottage communities, modest homes, and rentals. We talked about how different many parts of the Cape were from each other—from extreme wealth to poverty, to those in between.

I shared some Provincetown history, starting from the early Europeans to the thriving community it is today. A few settlers from Plymouth Colony were granted large sections of the Outer Cape, from Brewster to Truro. They designed their settlements to be outside of the Colony's strict Puritan orders. It was not until 1727 that Provincetown was incorporated, with the scrub forest and dunes being claimed by the colony. Over the next 100 years, the town grew and thrived through its fishing industry, eventually using up to 55 wharves and dozens of schooners.

Until incorporation, the Province Lands' Portuguese fishing community would take in single men to work and live in this "unincorporated" trade community. It thereby became a place for transients, smugglers, escaped indentured servants, and "mooncussers" (land-based pirates who would decoy signal lights on dark nights to cause shipwrecks for plundering). It wasn't until 1893 that the Massachusetts General Court allowed the residents of Provincetown to hold deeds to the land they'd been living on. For 166 years, P'towners were essentially squatters.

We stopped near the Provincetown town line to climb on a boardwalk over the dunes, letting the sun warm our faces and the breeze cool us. We were met there by a photographer from the *Cape Cod Times*, who took our photos for the story about the Camino Way that would run a few days later.

All summer I had struggled to balance the desire to have a walking pilgrimage that stayed true to the values of reflection and learning, but at the same time, let people know what we were doing to support social justice and anti-racist action. Being willing to share what I was learning, and providing the container for others to experience Cape Cod in a different way, was an important part of my own growth over the summer. As this was the last walk, the *Times'* coverage was a story about a Cape Codder developing a deeper understanding of the historical and current issues around racism and social justice. (A link to the *Cape Cod Times*, Aug. 26, 2020 article included in the Resources!)

As we crossed into Provincetown, we began our conversation about LGBTQ+ rights and issues, and how Provincetown became the artist colony and "gay mecca" that it is today. **Charles Webster Hawthorne** started the Cape Cod School of Art in Provincetown in 1899.

E. Ambrose Webster opened his Summer School of Painting the next year. Open-minded intellectuals from Greenwich Village began to flock to P'town, including gay painters **Marsden Hartley** and **Charles Demuth**. By the early 1910s, Provincetown had six art schools, with *The Boston Globe* calling the tip of Cape Cod the "Biggest Art Colony in the World."

In the early 1900s, the Cape Cod Pilgrim Memorial Association erected the Pilgrim Monument to commemorate the Pilgrims' first landing and signing of the Mayflower compact, a document that inspired our nation's values of freedom and tolerance. That is the official story. There is some speculation, however, that just as monuments to the veterans of the Civil War were being erected in the South to reinforce white supremacy, the Provincetown monument may have been connected with the intention of reinforcing the white settler narrative and white supremacy over the influx of Portuguese to the area.

Over the next 100 years, Provincetown certainly became an oasis for such freedom and tolerance. With its artist colony booming, actors and playwrights such as Eugene O'Neill and Tennessee Williams visited to write, be inspired, and hone their skills. The town's cultural offerings also grew to include gay bars, nude beaches, drag queens, Carnival, and everything else that makes Provincetown such a beacon of a "free" lifestyle.

The theme for the **Provincetown Tennessee Williams Theater Festival** that September 2020, was "Tennessee Williams & Censorship," presenting an outdoor, reduced season of some lesser-known Williams plays alongside work by other wayward writers. As Festival Curator David Kaplan puts it, the theme of Censorship honored not the Pilgrims' arrival, but their *leaving*, allowing for 400 years of independent thinking (what the Puritans called "flaunting") that continues today. Provincetown remains special today because of its freedom of expression and support for all people, including LGBTQ+ folks.

We walked on the beach, with the **Pilgrim Monument** like a beacon in the distance drawing us toward the town, and stopped for an iced coffee break. My friend Licia provided us with iced coffee, and then joined us for the remainder of the walk. We listened to excerpts from **poems by Nikki Giovanni**, a renowned Black poet I met at Virginia Tech about a decade ago and was incredibly inspired by. She is REAL.

"There is always something to do. There are hungry people to feed, naked people to clothe, sick people to comfort and make well. And while I don't expect you to save the world I do think it's not asking too much for you to love those with whom you sleep, share the happiness of those whom you call friend, engage those among you who are visionary and remove from your life those who offer you depression, despair and disrespect."

"Mistakes are a fact of life. It is the response to the error that counts."

"If you don't understand yourself you don't understand anybody else."

We continued our walk down Commercial St, passing many historic homes of visual and performing artists and writers, then met Wilderness and Saffron, joining for another walk, at the **Helping Our Women (HOW)** office on Conwell St. Chloe, a VISTA staff member at HOW, helped us to understand their importance as a resource, particularly during the pandemic, by giving us a tour and overview of the variety of their services available to women of the Outer Cape.

We walked across Rt 6, following Race Point Rd until we joined the Province Lands Bike Trail winding its way through **Beech Forest**. We spent time talking in pairs about what the experience of walking the Cape Cod Camino Way had meant to us, as we all had been on more than one walk over the summer. We all agreed the walks provided an outstanding way to learn more about the place where we lived, the people whose stories we had not heard before, and the facts that we needed to be informed about to move forward in new ways to do anti-racist work.

As we rounded the bend by Herring Cove Beach, we continued onto Province Lands Rd (the very end of Rt 6A) and headed toward the breakwater, with the Wood End Light in the distance. Knowing that we had walked from the Canal to the tip of the Cape was heart-warming for me. We stopped at **Pilgrim's First Landing Park** and gazed across to Long Point Light and the dunes in the distance. A reporter met us there to interview us for the *Cape Cod Times* article, and this provided a time for reflection with fellow walkers. We breathed in deeply the sea air and gave thanks for our time together.

Turning up Commercial St for the last time, I remembered being there in June, before the summer crowds, planning the Cape Cod Camino Way. I thought about the walkers and other participants (43 total) who joined me over the 100+ miles across Cape Cod during the past eight weeks. We looked up to the Pilgrim Monument and noted that the Provincetown Museum at its base now provided a more historically accurate account of the Pilgrims' time on Cape Cod. We ended our journey at the AIDS Memorial next to Town Hall, where we shared our sadness in the discrimination against LGBTQ+ people and the loss of so many people to AIDS.

Instead of a Closing Circle, due to the crowds, we decided to end our experience together over lunch outdoors at The Canteen. There, five of us continued our conversation about what next steps we as individuals, and in connection with others, would take on our exploration of racial and social justice. We recalled some of our experiences of the summer: examining our foundational documents of democracy, learning about the Wampanoag story, visiting the Zion Union Heritage Museum, walking the Labyrinth in Chatham, learning about the Cape economy and the Triangular Trade, exploring the natural environment, walking the beach into Provincetown, and sharing our personal stories with each other. We sighed, laughed, hugged, and expressed gratitude for the time we'd spent together over the summer, both in silent walking and in deep, impactful conversation.

> "There is so much more to know about our history and the heritage of Cape Cod (good and not so good) and the Cape Cod Camino Way project is one of the best ways to develop that knowledge while expanding community. Peggy is a scholar and a great leader of these events. She shares generously with her companions and provides a rich and diverse perspective on Cape Cod."
>
> -Robert Ross, Truro

A few of the ideas we discussed for future action included:

- Work to inspire others to undertake a similar project here on Cape Cod, or wherever they live.

- Share the knowledge gained this summer with others in our circles, including the Cape's school system for its incorporation into the curriculum.

- Speak up in situations where racist, sexist, homophobic, and other forms of hate speech are present, in order to educate with compassion.

- Continue to seek out a variety of sources of information, artists, writers, and musicians to increase awareness of a variety of perspectives and issues. Support the local arts community and advocate for cultural diversity across the arts.

- Communicate through a variety of outlets (newspapers, blogs, Facebook posts, etc.) what we had learned and experienced.

- Write a journal or travelogue about the experience of the Cape Cod Camino Way.

- Develop new, shorter routes to encourage more people to experience their own Cape Cod Camino Way.

- Partner with Black, Indigenous and People of Color to amplify their voices around issues of racial and social justice.

- Support local businesses and the arts owned or created by Black, Indigenous and People of Color.

- Seek out additional people, places, and stories on Cape Cod representing the experience of people of color, in particular Black, Indigenous, and Cape Verdean.

- With the 2020 election looming in the fall, work with local, state, and federal campaigns to support candidates seeking to advance social justice and an anti-racist agenda.

- Keep walking, keep learning.

For further discussion of next steps, please see additional reflections and actions in the final chapter.

Resources:

Cape Cod National Seashore
https://www.nps.gov/caco/index.htm
Cape School of Art
https://capeschoolofart.org/
"Capewide pilgrimage offers a fuller version of history" by Ethan Genter, *Cape Cod Times*, August 26, 2020
https://www.capecodtimes.com/story/news/2020/08/26/capewide-pilgrimage-offers-fuller-version-of-history/114070992/
Helping Our Women
https://helpingourwomen.org/
Pilgrim Monument and Provincetown Museum
https://www.pilgrim-monument.org/
Plimoth Patuxet Museums
https://www.plimoth.org/
Provincetown Art Association and Museum
https://www.paam.org/
Provincetown Tennessee Williams Theater Festival
https://www.twptown.org/
Truro Historical Society
https://trurohistoricalsociety.org/
Truro Public Library
https://trurolibrary.org/

Create Your Own Walk with Friends and Family

Any number of combinations exist for interesting walks in and around Provincetown.

Option 1: For a walk that focuses on the environment and nature, consider the Beech Forest walking trail or Province Lands Bike Trail, which can be accessed from any of the parking areas at Herring Cove, Race Point, or Beech Forest. All offer a variety of paths in both sun and shade. From Beech Forest, you can also access the dike path to Hatches Harbor, a remote walking experience across the outer dunes of the National Seashore. – Length varies depending on route

Option 2: To experience the history of the local area and the Pilgrims, consider touring the Pilgrim Monument and Provincetown Museum, then walking to Town Hall past the Veterans Memorial and AIDS Memorial, and out to MacMillan Pier. Then traverse Commercial St to the East End and the Provincetown Public Library to view the half-scale model of the Rose Dorothea schooner on the second floor, as well as the 30 works of art from the Town's Art Collection. Visit the Packard Gallery to learn about a significant art family in town, and visit the Provincetown Art Association and Museum to complete your cultural walk. – 2 miles

Option 3: Another option is to turn left when leaving MacMillan Pier, and continue on Commercial St to the West End of town, stopping at the Provincetown Bookshop for works by local authors, including many LGBTQ+ people and people of color. Continue down Commercial, passing by many historic homes of artists and fishing families, to reach Pilgrim's First Landing Park. If the tide is low and it's not too late in the day, walk the breakwater across the bay to Long Point Beach to reach the tip of Cape Cod. – 3 miles

Lessons Learned from the
Cape Cod Camino Way Walks

> *"I am and always will be a catalyst for change."*
> -Shirley Chisholm
>
> *"In the end, we will remember not the words of our enemies, but the silence of our friends."*
> -Dr. Martin Luther King, Jr.

Attempting to summarize a profoundly deep and life-changing time is like trying to take a bite of a rich, creamy piece of cake that you can't fit in your mouth, and leaves you wanting more. When I started planning this journey in May and June of 2020, I had no idea how each week would unfold, what routes we would take, who we would meet, or what we would learn. I started as an inquisitive, open-minded person wanting to experience the full breadth of stories the various people on the Cape, and Cape Cod itself, had to offer. I wanted to maintain a reflective posture towards the experience, taking my time to understand the context and complexity of the issues of racism and social justice in my own community as well as nationally.

I visited every town on Cape Cod, heard the stories of interesting local people, interacted on a deep level with issues such as policing, health care, the environment, the economy, and systemic racism. I was blessed to have over 40 people join me on one or more of the walks, or meet us to visit a historic site or speaker. Many people were inspired to walk more than one week.

Lauren walked all eight weeks with me, providing companionship and a sounding board for the exploration of everything we encountered. I am deeply indebted to my fellow walkers and every person who interacted with us along the way. share with you now the arc of the Cape Cod Camino Way experience through the lens of "reflection in action," a circular process of awareness leading to reflection, developing and taking action, learning, integration, and then more reflection.

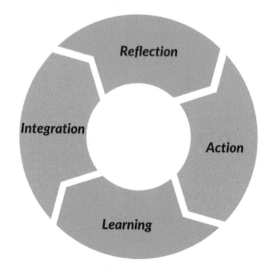

The reflection in action process I share below is adapted from the **21-Day Racial Equity Habit Building Challenge** developed by Dr. Eddie More, Jr. and Debby Irving.

Catalyst: Stress/Tension- Something is not right; My mind/body/spirit is uncomfortable; Events or people challenge me

The spring and early summer of 2020 saw an unprecedented series of major life and societal challenges facing Americans, including most of us on Cape Cod:

• The Covid-19 pandemic was rapidly spreading, threatening the health of most of the world. It had shut down the economy, wreaking havoc on every aspect of society. My work in higher education went online. We originally thought the pandemic would be over in a few months, but slowly realized we would be living with Covid implications for a very long time.

• The murders of George Floyd, Breonna Taylor, and Ahmaud Arbery, in addition to over 150 other Black people killed by police in the first 8 months of 2020, sparked protest activity nationally, including here on Cape Cod.

• The federal government, along with many states, refused to implement appropriate Covid mitigation strategies, making the impact of the pandemic worse with the U.S. leading in infection rates and deaths.

• The increasingly polarized legislative process in Congress and the 2020 election cycle of primaries led to the demonization of candidates and parties.

• The rise of conspiracy theory sources like QAnon paralleled an embracing of white supremacist rhetoric by the President, many federal and state leaders, and some American news outlets.

• A rise in the use of social media to spread false information on the virus, protest activity, the elections, and every other aspect of life.

• Social isolation led to an increase in mental health issues such as anxiety and depression, as well as domestic violence, addiction, and other mental health conditions.

• An inability to travel far distances and cancelled vacations opened up new considerations of local exploration.

• Those who may not have faced these challenges directly were still watching family and friends struggle to make sense of these endless, overlapping stressors.

1. Awareness- *Really listen, watch, scan the body, pay attention*

Over the course of 2020, I became obsessed with the national and local news, tuning into familiar and new sites to become aware of the various perspectives on critical issues. Each morning I spent over an hour on the *Cape Cod Times*, *New York Times*, *Fox News*, and Facebook websites collecting pieces of information and raising my stress level.

I listened to people of color through a variety of mediums: podcasts, movies, Facebook posts, interviews, and webinars from local, state, and national sources. I sought out information every day, and processed what I was learning with others. I always listened to a variety of voices and sources of information, and I doubled my effort to focus on voices of color.

In order to promote awareness and process what I was experiencing in my body, I recommitted to making a regular habit of **meditation** (walking beach meditation works the best for me) and yoga practice. I joined online yoga sessions from several studios on Cape Cod, and from my favorite retreat centers—Kripalu in the Berkshires, MA, and Suryalila in Spain. Seeking to increase my inner awareness of the extra stress' impact on my mind and body, I took my meditations to nature through long walks in forests and on the beach. I reaffirmed that **creating space and embracing practices to promote awareness and mindfulness enables one to gain valuable insights related to both the issues being explored, and to the "container" of oneself: mind, body, and spirit.** Too often in the past, I have moved directly from feeling tension or stress to taking action. Through employing techniques learned and practiced over the past decade (mindfulness, yoga, nature walks, journaling, etc.) I intentionally enabled deeper awareness and reflection to inform action.

2. Reflection- *What possibilities exist for me now?*

I have kept a journal, on and off, since college. I turned to the journal again, and my writing group, to explore current issues and anxieties, in particular those associated with race, social justice, and the pandemic. I would find myself writing in my car in the evenings at Paine's Creek Beach, watching the sun set on another day, feeling grateful to be given the chance to slow down and reflect. I was grateful to not be leading a large organization during the pandemic, and to be in the role of coach and consultant. I was grateful to have the time to germinate the Camino Way as a project to explore racism and other social justice issues close to home. And I reflected on my family and close friends, and how to be present in their lives during this difficult time.

3. Action- *What concrete steps did I take?*

I joined five other white women to read and discuss the book *White Fragility* by Robin DiAngelo. This led to us writing an editorial for the *Cape Cod Times* (see page [#]), which was itself a process of reflection and dialogue to create. We wanted to incorporate all voices and feedback, and made a conscious decision to have our names associated with anti-racism.

I tuned into Kathy Obear's trainings for forming and leading White Accountability Groups, while doing the deep individual work around my own racism and how to promote change and growth in myself and others. As a gifted trainer in higher education whom I have known for 35 years, Kathy provided the Zoom venue for hundreds of others around the country to explore how to consistently be anti-racist and lead accountability groups.

I planned to use the training to inform my Camino Way walks and discussions with people along the way.

I attended local protests in Barnstable and Orleans, where I laid face down in the grass for 8 minutes and 40 seconds of silence to honor George Floyd and realized just how long that time felt. I had taken part in protest activity in the past, primarily related to women's issues, starting in college and continuing over the years.

Watching the protest activity around the country, including some destruction of property and looting, caused me to have several difficult conversations about what it means to protest today, and what is "acceptable" through the lens of respectability and peaceful demonstrations I had aligned myself with in the past. I came to better understand the depth of anger and frustration voiced by Black, Indigenous and People of Color, and listened to their pain in a way I never had before.

Through my work at Bridgewater State University, and as a consultant in higher education, I was able to join several groups examining systems of oppression—equity and inclusion seminars, implicit bias trainings, and deep conversations with colleagues of color—to expand my knowledge base and deepen my understanding of what actions were necessary now. Like many "progressive" white administrators and faculty in higher education, I wanted to move further on the continuum of understanding towards action that would change and hold accountable our fundamental economic and social systems. I also began the work to change myself.

4. Understanding- *What am I learning? How does this align with or contradict what I have known to be true?*

The breadth and depth of my learning that occurred over the spring and summer of 2020 was profound. I would equate it to a semester or year in college, taking several impactful courses that filled me with new knowledge and awareness. Here are just a few of the understandings around issues of race and social justice that were deepened for me during 2020:

The Wampanoag story on Cape Cod is either woefully misunderstood, or not understood at all by the majority of the Cape's population, along with the rest of the country. Our education system, museums, cultural institutions, and tourism industry, just to name a few, still need to embrace the accurate history of the Native American people and celebrate their contributions. Only through sowing the seeds necessary for social and economic change can the destruction of thousands of Native American tribes' lands and way of life be repaid, and the hundreds of years of misinformation be corrected. This became more apparent to me week after week on the Camino Way walks where the "real story" of the Pilgrims and the Wampanoag continued to evolve over the 400th anniversary year of the Pilgrims' arrival.

The unsung contributions of women and people of color to many areas of our history—the economy, the arts, community organizations, education, religion, politics, etc.—became clearer to me as I researched each walk and shared my findings with those who walked with me or followed the Camino Way Project on Facebook. I recalled taking Dr. Joyce Berkman's Women's History class my senior year at UMass Amherst, after spending three years as an American History major in courses based on traditional Western and male perspectives. My eyes were opened by that course, and the process of walking Cape Cod forty years later harkened back to what I learned then: research alternative stories and sources, include the voices of those marginalized by the traditional narrative, expand the definition of what is important, and explore rabbit holes of new questions and knowledge. Once I had really looked around me, I realized there were women and people of color to be found in much of the Cape's history. These include women and people of color in the science community of Woods Hole, Black artists at the Zion Union Heritage Museum in Hyannis, and the Wampanoag histories of Mashpee, Chatham, and Wellfleet. And the artistic voices of women and people of color rang out through centuries of poetry, music, painting, theater, and more.

The issue of race in the United States, with the institution of slavery woven into the development of the North, became a powerful "understanding" for me. I knew that the North benefited from the work of the enslaved in the South, and I knew that Northerners, including those in Massachusetts, had enslaved both Native American and Black people. But I hadn't understood the full impact of the Northern economy's deeply entwined history (through trade, banking, insurance, politics, religion, etc.) with the institution of slavery.

The exploration of the cemeteries in my hometown of Brewster brought the Triangular Trade to life for me. The many resources at the end of this book (as well as each chapter) share some of the hundreds of sources about race (including the enslavement of Black people) that I was introduced to and tried to consume over the course of the year. I still have stacks of books and articles to read; podcasts to listen to; webinars and trainings to attend. This will be a never-ending opportunity for me to continue to expand my understanding of the roots of racism in this country, and determine what I must do personally, and in collaboration with others, to be anti-racist—to be part of the change.

On a personal level, the walks and conversations shared with the 40+ people who joined me on this journey touched me very deeply. First, my family. Through our commitment to unpack issues of racism and white privilege, either on the walks or through Zoom calls and in-person conversations, we came to understand each other better, support our individual growth and exploration, and celebrate our love for each other. Experiencing racism directed at family members enabled me to understand their feelings in a profound way. I felt their pain in my mind, body, and spirit. I deepened my commitment to continue this work on behalf of my niece, my sister-in-law, and their family from Trinidad. In addition, I reached out to numerous colleagues of color in higher education to check in with them, to let them know about the work I was doing with the Camino Way, and to offer them to join me in some way. Many did through the Facebook page, Zoom calls, and individual conversations. Again, many friendships were strengthened because I continued to do my own work, and because I listened to the stories of others in a different way than in the past.

One cannot help but become closer to the environment when one walks for days on end across the landscape of a particular area. I was already aware of climate change and supported the work of local organizations, such as the Association to Preserve Cape Cod, the conservation commissions, Cape Cod Museum of Natural History, and Mass Audubon. For decades I have visited by foot and bike many of the trails and sites in the Cape Cod National Seashore. To walk every week on the roads, bike paths, cartways, and nature trails across Cape Cod provided me, and others, the opportunity to connect deeply with environmental issues of serious importance. My understanding of the fragility of this peninsula, and of all aspects of nature found here, was strengthened. And my commitment to action, be it decreasing my use of plastics or support for wind energy, were inspired and acted upon.

5. Integration- *How do I need to change my behavior/approach to incorporate new perspectives and information?*

The process of integration is spherical, moving up and down and around at the same time. Taking what I was learning and experiencing on a weekly basis, and incorporating that new knowledge and understanding into both my personal and professional lives, was an integral part of the Camino Way journey. And it continues to be so. Once one commits to seeing and acting upon racism, one cannot "unsee it." One can choose to ignore or not act, but for me, awareness led to the action and integration necessary to enable me to speak up against racist behavior and actions, and speak out on behalf of the Black and Brown people around me.

I have a wide network of colleagues and friends from working at several colleges in my career, and from serving in higher education professional associations. I edited out some former friends and colleagues because their racist, classist, or homophobic behavior became intolerable to me. No longer being around them served me well. I should have moved on years earlier, and I did so now because it was the only thing to do. It is always hard to give something or someone up; but it is harder to keep harming oneself and providing support to racist ideology by staying in such a relationship.

I continued to ask questions, not assuming I knew the story of a particular historical account, or a group of people. By remaining open, inviting others to join me on a learning journey, the ongoing process of integration continues.

6. Remain hopeful- *Share insights with others; surround yourself with support.*

Over the course of the summer and fall of 2020, my sense of hope and positive change for the future grew immensely. It was tempered, however, by the election cycle; the demonizing of Black Lives Matter protesters by the President's actions and those of his followers and law enforcement; and the spread of misinformation to feed fear and anxiety. The pandemic was still ongoing, with "anti-science" and "anti-maskers" exercising their right to be wrong in various public forums. By decreasing my time on news and social media sites, I found I could feed my soul with more hopeful and accurate sources of information and support. When talking about the Camino Way, and the continued learning growing out of the project, I gave credit to the resilience of people of color over hundreds of years, remaining hopeful and strong in the face of severe adversity. By acknowledging their contributions as well as their pain over generations, I remained hopeful that, in spite of significant setbacks, progress had been made, and more would be possible with a new administration in January. I remained anxious yet hopeful as the presidency and the Senate turned away from the policies and people of the Trump-aligned party. I remained hopeful that moderate Republicans would emerge to challenge the dominant narrative.

Little did I know that any degree of hopefulness would be deeply challenged on January 6 with the insurrection at the Capitol Building that attempted to overturn the election and subvert the democratic process. Millions of people like me were outraged by the destruction of property, the threats on the lives of elected officials, and the injury and death of innocent people by the mob of angry partisans in support of an illegitimate cause connected with maintaining white supremacy. I remain hopeful because at the end of the day, the insurrection failed. But the decision of some Republicans to still challenge the election on the floor of the Senate, and then vote against convicting the former president for his role in inciting the violence, created a sense of anger and fear within me. But my resolve to continue to work to dismantle systems of oppression remained intact. I regained some measure of hopefulness through the Inauguration Day festivities, tearing up when **Amanda Gorman, the first National Youth Poet Laureate, performed her poem "The Hill We Climb" in front of the world:**

"When day comes we ask ourselves,
where can we find light in this never-ending shade?"

"But while democracy can be periodically delayed,
it can never be permanently defeated."

In her words, America "isn't broken, but simply unfinished." Thank you, Amanda Gorman, for giving us hope! In watching Vice President Harris and her husband, Second Gentleman Doug Emhoff, in turn watch the fireworks boom above the Lincoln Memorial, I saw what the future could look like. Like many on that Inauguration Day, I could exhale and move forward.

I remain hopeful because I had interacted with people from all backgrounds over the 2020 summer who were also seeking awareness and understanding for themselves. I saw that many people were open to hearing perspectives they were not aware of, interacting with others who were different from them, and committing to incorporating their understanding into positive anti-racist action.

I remain hopeful because I know that the work I did in 2020 inspired others to take action in similar ways, right where they live. I continue to encourage and support individual and group action for creating similar projects like the Camino Way around the region of wherever people live and call home. I will continue to explore issues of racial and social justice on Cape Cod, and will offer shorter, more accessible walks for a wider audience. I will also offer to speak about the Camino Way experience, and creating similar projects for learning, with organizations and institutions here on Cape Cod and across the country. I am hopeful that by sharing my experience through this book, the Facebook page, inspirational talks, and new walks during the Summer of 2021, I model for others possible ways of seeking opportunities to learn and challenge oneself to grow and take action for change.

I remain hopeful because I have seen tangible examples of young people reaching across the divides of race, gender, and class identities to forge alliances, support the systemic work that needs to be done, and become true allies.

I remain hopeful as I see museum exhibits and curriculum in schools address the stories and perspectives of people of color. I see churches exploring reparations for past ministers who owned enslaved people. I see towns struggling through the reckoning of racist symbols used by their schools and sports teams. I see arts organizations embrace a wider array of artists and genres in their programming.

I remain hopeful because I reaffirmed my love for Cape Cod and deepened my desire to make it a better place for all of the people who live here.

Finally, I remain hopeful for new partnerships with others doing similar work to bear fruit. The work is difficult and monumental; only through collaborations and partnerships will progress be sustained. Now that my thirst for knowledge and understanding has been stoked to a blaze, I need to continue to interrogate a variety of aspects of my experience, and commit to being part of the change.

Keep walking, keep learning! It's the only way for me.

Resources:
21-Day Challenge's Recommended Resources
https://www.debbyirving.com/recommended-resources/
21-Day Racial Equity Habit Building Challenge
www.eddiemoorejr.com/21daychallenge
The Center for Transformation and Change created by Dr. Kathy Obear
https://drkathyobear.com/
"The Hill We Climb" by Amanda Gorman, spoken at the 2021 Presidential Inauguration
https://www.youtube.com/watch?v=LZO55illiN4

Epilogue
Civil Rights and Civil War Tour

Once one becomes open, opportunities for learning and engagement abound. Every place of travel becomes a canvas to explore: whose stories do I need to understand here? What is the experience of people of color in this space and over time? What do I need to see, to hear, to feel, and to experience fully?

In January of 2021, I decided to work remotely from Florida and structure two opportunities for continuing the Camino Way walks through the American South. Driving alone in the South as a single woman of liberal background and an eye toward interrogating the traditional narrative, I sought out places and experiences that would both inform and challenge me. Each place I stopped offered not only the "expected" site or learning, but something additional to explore, unexpected findings, and experiences that continued to feed my quest for knowledge and understanding.

A few of the more poignant examples are shared below to encourage you to use opportunities for travel (even short local trips!) to inquire about the experience of those not immediately apparent, those left out of the traditional historical narrative. I hope that you find, like me, your travels enriched, lively, sometimes uncomfortable, but always worth the effort when exploring the "other story."

Civil Rights & Civil War Tour

Brewster, MA
Richmond, VA
Chapel Hill, NC
St. Augustine, FL
Fort Myers, FL
Mobile, AL
Montgomery, AL
Birmingham, AL
Chattanooga, TN
Cherokee, NC
Asheville, NC
Christiansburg, VA
Lexington, VA
Harpers Ferry, WV
Gettysburg, PA
Manhattan, NY
Stonington, CT
Brewster, MA

Part I. The Drive to Florida

January 25 – 30 (5 days)
Stopping in Richmond, VA; Chapel Hill, NC; and St. Augustine, FL

About 15 years ago, I first visited Richmond, VA, and received a tour of Monument Avenue from a descendent of the first white Virginia settlers. I remember at the time feeling that the extreme size of the monuments, their placement on a prominent main avenue, and their continued glorification of the Civil War was offensive. When I stopped there in late January, 2021, I found the statues themselves had been removed, and their pedestals and bases covered in Black Lives Matter-related graffiti. Fences surrounded the Robert E. Lee statue. As I stood there in the cold wind, with no people walking the grand avenue, I was struck by the messages of anger, pain, frustration, and also love that were left to weather through the winter. Similarly, when I walked the University of North Carolina campus in Chapel Hill, I saw the site of the former confederate statue, "Silent Sam." Nearby in McCorkle Place was the Unsung Founders Memorial dedicated to the enslaved people who helped build the university, but it felt inadequate, just as it did in 2005 when we dedicated it.

How were Richmond, Chapel Hill, and other Southern cities going to resolve the ongoing conflicts over the monuments and symbols of the Confederacy in particular, and racism in general, that pervade their public spaces? What stories would be told in the future through the removal of the current symbols, and installation of other underrepresented works? How does a community, a government, an organization like a college or hospital deal with the legacy, expressed either implicitly or explicitly, of founders with racist or oppressive histories?

We do not have a good track record of "truth and reconciliation" processes in the United States. I remembered meeting Archbishop Desmond Tutu at the University of North Carolina years ago, and his message to the graduates to both interrogate and forgive. We have to go back and relearn what we don't know about our collective past; to create a structured process of responsibility and accountability in which individuals and organizations can engage. I hope that in some way the work of the Camino Way can be part of that process.

A few days later I found myself taking a break in my travels in St. Augustine, FL. With a few free hours to spend before meeting a friend for dinner, I literally stumbled upon the Black Heritage Trail, which weaves its way around the town to bring attention to Black landmarks and historical places of interest. I was astounded that, without seeking out this trail, it had presented itself to me! I enjoyed learning how St. Augustine, one of the oldest cities in the United States, had a rich, thriving Black culture spanning several hundred years—Fort Mose, located just two miles north of the city, was the first legally sanctioned community of free Black people in America.

I would find other such trails throughout the South, some well-marked like that of Mobile, AL, and others hidden, like that of Fort Myers, FL. By asking, "Where are the stories of people of color in this particular landscape?" I was able to enrich my travels through learning about others and seeing places off the typical tourist map. The information I learned would continue to inform my social justice work.

Part II. The Drive Back North

Early April, 2021 (12 days)
Stopping in Mobile, Montgomery, and Birmingham, AL; Chattanooga, TN; Cherokee, NC; Lexington, VA; the Shenandoah Valley; Harper's Ferry, WV; Gettysburg, PA; and Stonington, CT

While in Florida, I decided to leave two weeks earlier than planned to embark on a Civil Rights/Civil War learning experience through the heart of the protest activity of the 1960s, Confederacy and Civil War sites, and places where I could experience history from a variety of perspectives. Every place I went had one or two typical sites to see and learn from, but the deeper engagement occurred when I went off the beaten path to explore the "alternative" routes and narratives, and explicitly asked "where are the historical sites related to people of color." By remaining open to seeing what was right in front of me, I was able to interact with perspectives and ideas that both informed and challenged me. I always felt safe, and people went out of their way to be of assistance to me.

In Mobile, AL, I walked part of the Dora Franklin Finley African-American Heritage Trail, which includes dozens of sites related to the history of Black people in Mobile. I found heartbreaking stories, such as that of Michael Donald Avenue, the street on which its namesake was murdered, making him the last Black man lynched in the United States and the cause of the bankruptcy of the Ku Klux Klan. Another story I encountered in Mobile was the Slave Market where thousands of Africans were sold as property to Southern planters.

There were honors to Satchel Paige, the oldest player in major league baseball, and Hank Aaron, for his 33-year-long record for most home runs. As a life-long Red Sox baseball fan, I remembered that the Red Sox, like the Celtics and other Boston area sports teams, had a troubled history of integration.

I spent two days in Mobile, exploring the History Museum of Mobile's exhibit chronicling its troubled past of racism, numerous integrated and segregated churches, and college campuses, such as University of South Alabama and Spring Hill College, that continue to explore their connections with white supremacy. One of the most disturbing photos I saw on my journey was that of a line of Klansmen marching into the Wesley Chapel United Methodist Church, and again was reminded of the connection between white supremacy and religion. In the Cathedral-Basilica of the Immaculate Conception are some of the oldest records of baptisms, marriages, and burials of the French, Spanish, British, Native American, African, and Creoles de Color in the South. I also learned that Mobile was the birthplace of Mardi Gras, started by Joe Cain, his fictitious "Chickasaw" chief character, and his "Lost Cause Minstrels," referring to the defeated Southland. I had no idea about the origins of Mardi Gras beyond the usual partying in New Orleans before the beginning of Lent. I could have spent a week in Mobile, but the rest of Alabama was calling.

I ventured north to Montgomery, where I found Jefferson Davis, the first President of the Confederacy, still standing by the steps of the Capitol, and the largest Confederate monument I had seen to date. I found numerous historical markers from the Alabama Historical Association at places of significance: the courthouses where major civil rights rulings took place, the Dexter Avenue King Memorial Baptist Church where Dr. Martin Luther King, Jr. preached, the train station depot where the enslaved were shipped, the memorial to Rosa Parks and the other women who took action to integrate public transportation, the Selma to Montgomery National Historic Trail, and new stone memorials across from the Capitol that told of the story of emancipation, reconstruction, and the Civil War in a compelling way. All of these sites helped to prepare me for my tour of the Civil Rights Memorial Center (which curates outstanding exhibits to enhance understanding) and the National Memorial for Peace and Justice honoring "the legacy of enslaved Black people, people terrorized by lynching, African Americans humiliated by racial segregation and Jim Crow, and people of color burdened with contemporary presumptions of guilt and police violence. Nothing had quite prepared me for the visceral pain I felt while walking through the memorial's sculptures dedicated to the thousands of Black people murdered by white people. Row upon row of hanging plates honor the names of over 4,000 individuals killed, and include the county in which the lynching occurred.

The counties listed are from across the country. I found myself standing beneath Chatham County, NC, where I had lived for 6 years, and read the 6 names listed out loud, and cried. I heard a voice from within say, "You must do more," and I responded, "I will do more." It being Good Friday, I found a nearby labyrinth and walked in peace, breathing deeply for the forgiveness and strength to move forward.

Up the road in Birmingham, I went to the Birmingham Civil Rights Heritage Trail to walk the park where water cannons and dogs were unleashed on Civil Rights marchers, including children. The 16th Street Baptist Church stands sentinel on the corner of the park, honoring the four girls murdered in the bombing. As I reflected on this holy place, I read Martin Luther King's "Letter from a Birmingham Jail," a call to his white clergy colleagues to take action, though they did not.

I thought about the Black Lives Matter protests against ongoing killings of Black and Brown people, and how we need to continue to raise our voices for change. I was deeply moved and inspired by what I saw in Birmingham, grateful for the dedication of thousands who put their lives on the line to protest injustice. On my drive to Chattanooga, I listened to the trial of Derek Chauvin, the officer who murdered George Floyd, and was reminded of the symmetry of present-day police shootings to the lives taken during the Civil Rights Movement decades ago with no accountability or justice. I hoped for a different outcome this time.

On my travels from Tennessee to North Carolina, I spent some time exploring Cherokee, NC, and its surroundings, reminding myself of the thousands of years that Native Americans lived in peace before white settlers forced them off their lands.

I thought about how state and federal officials continue to treat the tribes with disrespect and violence. I hiked some of the trails nearby, where many Cherokees fled to form settlements and, through persistence, have created communities and a homeland that are a testament to the resilience of the Cherokee people.

In Asheville, NC, I found the thriving college community I remembered from over a decade ago, and enjoyed a day to regroup and integrate my learning and experiences (golf and yoga in botanical gardens will help with that). I found it important to practice some self-care along the way so I could absorb and manage the deep feelings being lodged in my mind, body, and spirit from all I was seeing and experiencing. I was reminded that people of color experience similar feelings of anger, frustration, fear, and pain every day. I gained a deeper understanding of the importance of supporting self-care for communities of color.

I next ventured into the heart of the former Confederacy to visit the campuses of Washington and Lee University and the Virginia Military Institute (VMI), located adjacent to each other in Lexington, VA. I found examples of Robert E. Lee and Stonewall Jackson, both prominent Confederate Generals, woven into the very fabric of the colleges and the town. Lee was elected to the vestry of the Grace Episcopal Church. I recalled that it took a Supreme Court case in 1996 to permit women to attend VMI. I learned that the Corps of Cadets, some of them mere teenagers, were called into battle during the Civil War, where most were injured and several died.

Washington and Lee benefited from the gifted estate of John Robinson, which included 74 enslaved men and women. Outside the main administration building I found the display, *"Difficult, Yet Undeniable, History,"* documenting the college's involvement with the institution of slavery, including the names of the enslaved who were owned by the college. I thought that this was a start at acknowledging the past. The first Black students would not enroll at Washington and Lee until 1966. I understand a commission is looking at renaming the college, and know that will be a tall task given its history and the perspective of many prominent alumni.

A local historian suggested I visit the town of New Market and the Virginia Museum of the Civil War. I'm glad I did. I was confronted immediately by the "white-washed" version of the Civil War as told from the perspective of the Virginia Military Institute and their cadets. I found souvenirs including a pink child's military cap emblazoned with the crossed swords of the Confederacy. I listened to the museum's movie that passionately recounts the young VMI men being called to service and dying on the battlefield outside. But what I found most compelling was touring the farm buildings in New Market where the battle took place, and found the outbuilding where those enslaved lived.

And when I stumbled upon the disassembled monument to Stonewall Jackson on the field behind the museum, I gasped at the story strewn about the grass in front of me.

I thought back to Richmond in January and wondered where the statues of the generals had been taken. Now I saw where one from the VMI was placed out of sight in a field, lost to future generations to explore the meaning and context of its creation.

I continued on to one of my most surprising stops in two weeks: **Harpers Ferry, WV**. I knew the story of Harpers Ferry from history, and how **abolitionist John Brown sought to initiate a "slave rebellion" by taking over the national armory located in the town.** And I knew the Appalachian Trail crossed there at the junction of the two rivers, and enjoyed a walk from West Virginia to Maryland on a few miles of the trail.

In the year of Covid, I committed to walk the Appalachian Trail virtually, and was thrilled to actually get on a few miles of the actual trail. What I didn't know, however, was the story of Storer College, founded north of the historic town of Harpers Ferry right after the Civil War. **Storer College was one of the first colleges open to Black students, as well as to both male and female students, and thrived for many years until the 1950s.**

In 1905 a group of African Americans led by W.E.B. Du Bois met at Niagara Falls to demand equal rights for all people. In 1906, the group met again at Storer College, and Du Bois addressed those gathered: "We claim for ourselves every single right that belongs to a freeborn American, political, civil, and social; and until we get these rights we will never cease to protest and assail the ears of America. The battle we wage is not for ourselves alone but for all true Americans." Du Bois and others would go on to play a role in the formation of the National Association for the Advancement of Colored People, now known better as the NAACP.

I was astounded at what I had found in Harpers Ferry: a dozen abandoned Storer College buildings awaiting restoration and reclamation of their rightful place on the stage of civil rights history. I spent many unplanned hours walking this town, resting on the site of the former campus, and soaking in this unexpected find on my long journey home.

Gettysburg, PA, was astounding in its complexity while overwhelming in its glorification of war and death. The museum and battlefield itself consume hours of one's time and vast amounts of energy to take in the thousands of monuments, markers, obelisks, statues, and battle sites. What I found most remarkable, however, was the juxtaposition of these historic sites with the small, barely marked or cared for Lincoln Cemetery, established in 1867 for the burial of the African American citizens and Civil War veterans. These "Colored Troops" were denied burial in the National Cemetery due to segregation policies in place at the time.

The Lincoln Cemetery was located next to the emergency entrance of the town's major hospital! I could not help but find the incredulity of this situation. Why was this place barely marked or cared for by the Pennsylvania Historical and Museum Commission? Why were these veterans of color still in barely marked graves when there are monuments all around Gettysburg to white veterans?

In the Gettysburg Museum & Visitors Center I also saw symbols that were present at the Capitol insurrection in January: Confederate flags, flags with serpents and the words "unite or die," images of violence with swords and shields, battle uniforms, religious symbols, and faces filled with anger. After driving for miles through its monuments and battle fields, Gettysburg left me feeling exhausted from confronting the present rooted in the past. Our democratic institutions, from the press to the courts, are under attack. How will we withstand this new "civil war?" How will we move forward to fully integrate the history I was experiencing, and rectify the current inequities across all aspects of society? I had to keep driving, and while I tuned into an NPR story on race in the United States, I tried to remain hopeful.

Part III. Next Steps

This trip was powerful. It was intentional, with the purpose of continuing the Camino Way walks to expose me to history and context I needed to understand. I learned so much more than the facts and circumstances of a particular town or area of the country, or time period in history. I learned that I could put together a driving tour during a pandemic by myself, and navigate through the Deep South and be welcomed, both by the places and people who inhabit them. I did confront a few situations where, in order to conserve my energy, I chose not to engage with supporters of the former President and his false narrative. Self-care was a priority along the way home.

After having this experience, I am more convinced of my calling to explore the history and stories of where I live on Cape Cod, and to share what I am learning with others. I am also being called to stand up and speak out when I see racism in action, to take action to interrupt and challenge the situation. I'm being called to be an ally every day and in every way that I am afforded the opportunity, be it in my family life, in my work, and in my community. And I am being called to continue to explore new areas of the United States for their particular stories of race and social justice issues in a way that informs my work and my life moving forward. Keep walking, keep learning. That's just what I'm going to do!

NOTE: On April 20, 2021, Derek Chauvin was found guilty of murder and manslaughter in the death of George Floyd. Accountability and a step toward justice was made. Within 48 hours of the verdict, however, several Black and Brown people would be shot by the police, resulting in more deaths from institutionalized racism. More trauma, more pain. So much more work to be done. Be the change we want to see!

General References to Explore Social and Racial Justice

NOTE: There are thousands of resources for you to engage with as you expand your understanding of social and racial justice. These represent just a few that were helpful to me in 2020 as I explored the Cape Cod Camino Way. I encourage you to pick 2 or 3, and to be open to where your growing awareness takes you. There is so much more to learn!

Reading & Listening

21-Day Racial Equity Habit Building Challenge created by Dr. Eddie Moore, Jr. Join a group or engage on your own for 21 days to further your understanding of power, privilege, oppression, and equity. It's helpful to participate in a group with others and hold each other accountable.

The 1619 Project created by Nikole Hannah-Jones, *The New York Times Magazine*. Historical context for understanding the foundation of the United States, Slavery, and their continuing impact today.

"Ally or co-conspirator?: What it means to act #InSolidarity" by Alicia Garza. Shares ineffective and effective ways to be in solidarity.

Braiding Sweetgrass by Robin Wall Kimmerer. Outstanding exploration of science, nature, and Native American culture.

"The Case for Reparations" by Ta-Nehisi Coates, *The Atlantic*. Explains how reparations entail much more than enslavement.

Caste: The Origins of Our Discontents by Isabel Wilkerson. Understanding the meaning of "caste" in the American context and its continuing impact today.

"Explaining White Privilege to a Broke White Person" by Gina Crosley-Corcoran. Explores where race and class do and don't intersect.

How to Be an Antiracist by Ibram X. Kendi. Essential text for understanding motivation and action around anti-racism to enable productive and non-harmful action.

How White People Got Made by Quinn Norton. Explores where the term "white people" comes from and which ethnic groups have and have not been able to become "white" through U.S. history.

In It For the Long Haul: Overcoming Burnout and Passion Fatigue as Social Justice Change Agents by Kathy Obear. Her book and website has numerous valuable resources for individuals and organizations.

The New Jim Crow: Mass Incarceration in the Age of Colorblindness by Michelle Alexander. Deeply impactful work on the racism of the criminal justice system and what needs to change. See also her *New York Times* article, "The Injustice of This Moment Is Not an 'Aberration'.

On Being, a podcast hosted by Krista Tippett. Numerous episodes, including one with Resmaa Menakem, that provide context for race and social justice issues.

Stamped from the Beginning: The Definitive History of Racist Ideas in America by Ibram X. Kendi. Provides the historical and cultural framework of racism in order to rewrite the traditional/white narrative.

Talking about Race, Smithsonian National Museum of African American History and Culture. Race – and racism – has grown adept at shapeshifting to maintain power and privilege for some and suffering and oppression for others. To begin to dismantle racism and inequity, many things must happen simultaneously: historical understanding, community building, personal reflection, and committed anti-racist practice. This is a rich website with numerous learning modules.

Teaching Tolerance, Learning for Justice's magazine. Numerous issues exploring white supremacy violence, racism, education, and legal systems in need of change.

White Fragility: Why It's So Hard for White People to Talk About Racism by Robin DiAngelo. Foundational text for many white people to understand the history of racism.

"White Privilege: Unpacking the Invisible Knapsack" and other essays by Peggy McIntosh. Foundational work from 1989 for understanding "whiteness."

Watching

13th directed by Ava DuVernay, Netflix. A documentary about the connection between the U.S. institution of slavery and the present-day mass incarceration system. (1 hour 40 minutes)

Hamilton by Lin-Manuel Miranda. A filmed version of the original cast of the hit Broadway musical. (2 hours 40 minutes)

In the White Man's Image, PBS. A documentary about the Native American boarding school movement designed to "kill the Indian and save the man." (56 minutes)

Just Mercy directed by Destin Daniel Cretton, Warner Brothers. (2 hours 17 minutes)

The Reunited States directed by Ben Rekhi. A documentary that follows a young conservative couple and their children visiting every state during 2019-2020, and how their trip changes them. (1 hour 25 minutes)

Slavery by Another Name directed by Sam Pollard, PBS. A documentary that challenges the idea that slavery ended with the Emancipation Proclamation. (90 minutes)

Unnatural Causes...is inequality making us sick?, California Newsreel. A seven-part documentary series exploring racial and socioeconomic inequalities in health and U.S. healthcare. (4 hours total, episodes have variable lengths)

NOTE:

Please refer to each chapter for specific resources on racial and social justice on Cape Cod and in New England.

Margaret (Peggy) Jablonski is an organizational consultant and coach who specializes in managing change, leadership development, and building effective organizations. Peggy works with colleges, nonprofits, and small businesses to foster a culture of success, develop authentic leaders, and strengthen diverse teams through interactive retreats, workshops, and individual coaching experiences. With two decades of consulting experience, she has guided faculty and staff from dozens of colleges to advance change, improve services, and implement transformational programs.

Dr. Jablonski served higher education as an administrator and faculty member over four decades, including as Vice Chancellor for Student Affairs at UNC Chapel Hill, Dean for Campus Life at Brown University, and Dean for Residential and Campus Life at MIT. Peggy pursued teaching full-time at the graduate level in the School of Education at the University of Massachusetts, serving on the committee to develop a new doctoral curriculum in educational leadership. She also held adjunct faculty positions during her time in North Carolina at UNC Chapel Hill and NC State. Her research interests include women and leadership, organizational change, and the spiritual development.

Peggy's service to the field of education includes four years as the Editor of the *NASPA Journal* and leadership roles on the Regional and National Boards of the *National Association for Student Personnel Administrators*. Peggy served as Co-Editor of the NASPA monograph on dealing with campus violence after the Virginia Tech incident. A current member of the International Women's Forum and the MA chapter, she continues to mentor women and men in higher education across the country.

Dr. Jablonski has presented at many national and international conferences on a variety of topics including leadership, campus safety and crisis response, fundraising, and scholarship in student affairs. She was the keynote speaker at the Irish Student Services conference, and served on the Quality Assurance Review team for the National University of Ireland- Maynooth. A dual citizen of Ireland, Peggy enjoys international travel and learning experiences in a variety of cultures. Locations of recent retreats and educational programs include Morocco, Peru, Costa Rica, England, Ireland, Trinidad, Cuba, and Spain.

Peggy's service includes the Boards of the United Way and Habitat for Humanity, her membership on the Community Preservation Committee in Brewster, and fundraising for many women's organizations. She currently lives on Cape Cod and volunteers with a variety of organizations and causes. Peggy recently pursued her interest in yoga to become certified as a yoga instructor, combining Eastern and Western approaches to healthy living. She also completed certification for coaching through the Gestalt Center, Strengths Coach training, and is a member of the International Coaching Federation. An avid golfer, Peggy seeks to integrate yoga practices into the golfing experience.

Peggy's latest endeavor in 2020 created the Cape Cod Camino Way Project to examine issues of racial and social justice on Cape Cod. This subsequent book and her weekly walks on Cape Cod continue to inform her work on equity and inclusion in organizations.

Jablonski Consulting Group: Jablonskigroup.com
Capecodcaminoway.com
Pegjab@gmail.com

which had fallen to his share when the great repartition of land had taken place. He operated also the largest dairy farm in the country, furnishing milk and butter and cheese to every charitable institution, orphans' home, insane asylum, reform school and workhouse in the country, and getting just twice the prices for them that any other dairy farm would have asked. He also owned a great aguacate hacienda; he controlled the army; he controlled a powerful bank; the president of the Republic made no appointments to any office without his advice. He fought counter-revolution and political corruption, daily upon the front pages of twenty newspapers he had bought for that very purpose. He employed thousands of peons. As an employer, he would understand what don Genaro was contending with. As an honest revolutionist, he would know how to handle that dirty, bribe-taking little judge. "I'll go to see Velarde," said don Genaro in a voice gone suddenly flat, as if he despaired or was too bored with the topic to keep it up any longer. He sat back and looked at his guests bleakly. Everyone said something, it did not matter what. The episode of the morning now seemed very far away and not worth thinking about.

Uspensky sneezed with his hands over his face. He had spent two early morning hours standing up to his middle in the cold water of the horse fountain, with

had theories about speed, its use and abuse. He loved to explain that man, if he had concentrated on his spiritual development, as he should have done, would never have needed to rely on mechanical aids to conquer time and space. In the meantime, he admitted that he himself, who could communicate telepathically with anyone he chose, and who had once levitated himself three feet from the ground by a simple act of the will, found a great deal of pleasurable stimulation in the control of machinery. I knew something about his pleasure in driving an automobile. He had for one thing a habit of stepping on the accelerator and bounding across tracks before approaching trains. Speed, he said, was "modern" and it was everyone's duty to be as modern as one's means allowed. I surmised from Betancourt's talk that don Genaro's wealth allowed him to be at least twice as modern as Betancourt. He could afford high-powered automobiles that simply frightened other drivers off the road before him; he was thinking of an airplane to cut distance between the hacienda and the capital; speed and lightness at great expense was his ideal. Nothing could move too fast for don Genaro, said Betancourt, whether a horse, a dog, a woman or something with metal machinery in it. Doña Julia smiled approvingly at what she considered praise of her husband and, by pleasant inference, of herself.

There came a violent commotion along the hall, at the door, in the room. The servants separated, fell back, rushed forward, scurried to draw out a chair, and don Genaro entered, wearing Mexican country riding dress, a gray buckskin jacket and tight gray trousers strapped under the boot. He was a tall, hard-bitten, blue-eyed young Spaniard, stringy-muscled, thin-lipped, graceful, and he was in a fury. This fury he expected us to sympathize with; he dismissed it long enough to greet everybody all around, then dropped into his chair beside his wife and burst forth, beating his fist on the table.

It seemed that the imbecile village judge refused to let him have Justino. It seemed there was some crazy law about criminal negligence. The law, the judge said, does not recognize accidents in the vulgar sense. There must always be careful inquiry based on suspicion of bad faith in those nearest the victim. Don Genaro gave an imitation of the imbecile judge showing off his legal knowledge. Floods, volcanic eruptions, revolutions, runaway horses, smallpox, train wrecks, street fights, all such things, the judge said, were acts of God. Personal shootings, no. A personal shooting must always be inquired into severely. "All that has nothing to do with this case, I told him," said don Genaro. "I told him, Justino is my peon, his family have lived for three hundred years on our hacienda, this is MY business. I know what hap-

pened and all about it, and you don't know anything and all you have to do with this is to let me have Justino back at once. I mean today, tomorrow will not do, I told him." It was no good. The judge wanted two thousand pesos to let Justino go. "Two thousand pesos!" shouted don Genaro, thumping on the table; "try to imagine that!"

"How ridiculous!" said his wife with comradely sympathy and a glittering smile. He glared at her for a second as if he did not recognize her. She gazed back, her eyes flickering, a tiny uncertain smile in the corners of her mouth where the rouge was beginning to melt. Furiously he ignored her, shook the pause off his shoulders and hurried on, turning as he talked, hot and blinded and baffled, to one and another of his audience. It was not the two thousand pesos, it was that he was sick of paying here, paying there, for the most absurd things; every time he turned around there at his elbow was some thievish politician holding out his paw. "Well. there's one thing to do. If I pay this judge there'll be no end to it. He'll go on arresting my peons every time one of them shows his face in the village. I'll go to Mexico and see Velarde. . . ."

Everybody agreed with him that Velarde was the man to see. He was the most powerful and successful revolutionist in Mexico. He owned two pulque haciendas

Stepanov and the camera balanced on the small stone ledge, directing a scene which he was convinced could be made fron no other angle. He had taken cold; he now swallowed a mouthful of fried beans, drank half a glass of beer at one gulp, and slid off the long bench. His too-large striped overalls disappeared in two jumps through the nearest door. He went as if he were seeking another climate.

"He has a fever," said Andreyev. "If he does not feel better tonight we must send for Doctor Volk."

A large lumpish person in faded blue overalls and a flannel shirt inserted himself into a space near the foot of the table. He nodded to nobody in particular, and Betancourt punctiliously acknowledged the salute.

"You do not even recognize him?" Betancourt asked me in a low voice. "That is Carlos Montaña. You find him changed?"

He seemed anxious that I should find Carlos much changed. I said I supposed we had all changed somewhat after ten years. Besides, Carlos had grown a fine set of whiskers. Betancourt's glance at me plainly admitted that I, like Carlos, had changed and for the worse, but he resisted the notion of change in himself. "Maybe," he said, unwillingly, "but most of us, I think, for the better. It's poor Carlos. It's not only the whiskers, and the fat. He has, you know, become a failure."

"A Puss Moth," said don Genaro to Stepanov. "I flew it half an hour yesterday; awfully *chic*. I may buy it. I need something really fast. Something light, too, but it must be fast. It must be something I can depend upon at any minute." Stepanov was an expert pilot. He excelled in every activity that don Genaro respected. Don Genaro listened attentively while Stepanov gave him some clear sensible advice about airplanes: what kind to buy, how to keep them in order, and what one might expect of airplanes as a usual thing.

"Airplanes!" said Kennerly, listening in. "I wouldn't go up with a Mexican pilot for all the money in—"

"Airplane! At last!" cried doña Julia, like a gently enraptured child. She leaned over the table and called in Spanish softly as if waking someone, "Carlos! Do you hear? Genarito is going to buy me an airplane, after all!"

Don Genaro talked on with Stepanov as if he had not heard.

"And what will you do with it?" asked Carlos, eyes round and amiable from under his bushy brows. Without lifting his head from his hand, he went on eating his fried beans and green chile sauce with a spoon, good Mexican country fashion, and enjoying them.

"I shall turn somersaults in it," said doña Julia.

"A Failure," Betancourt went on, in English, which

Carlos could not understand, "though I must say he looks worse today than usual. He slipped and hurt himself in the bathtub this morning." It was as if this accident were another point against Carlos, symbolic proof of the fatal downward tendency in his character.

"I thought he had composed half the popular songs in Mexico," I said. "I heard nothing but his songs here, ten years ago. What happened?"

"Ah, that was ten years ago, don't forget. He does almost nothing now. He hasn't been director of the Jewel for, oh, ages!"

I observed the Failure. He seemed cheerful enough. He was beating time with the handle of his spoon and humming a song to Andreyev, who listened, nodding his head. "Like that, for two measures," said Carlos in French, "then like this," and he beat time, humming. "Then this for the dance. . . ." Andreyev hummed the tune and tapped on the table with his left forefinger, his right hand waving slightly. Betancourt watched them for a moment. "He feels better just now, poor fellow," he said, "now I have got him this job. It may be a new beginning for him. But he is sometimes tired, he drinks too much, he cannot always do his best."

Carlos had slumped back in his chair, his round shoulders drooped, his swollen lids covered his eyes, he poked fretfully at his plate of enchiladas with sour cream.

"You'll see," he said to Andreyev in French, "how Betancourt will not like this idea either. There will be something wrong with it. . . ." He said it not angrily, not timidly, but with an unhappy certainty. "Either it will not be modern enough, or not enough in the old style, or just not Mexican enough. . . . You'll see."

Betancourt had spent his youth unlocking the stubborn secrets of Universal Harmony by means of numerology, astronomy, astrology, a formula of thought-transference and deep breathing, the practice of will-to-power combined with the latest American theories of personality development; certain complicated magical ceremonies; and a careful choice of doctrines from the several schools of Oriental philosophies which are, from time to time, so successfully introduced into California. From this material he had constructed a Way of Life which could be taught to anyone, and once learned led the initiate quietly and surely toward Success: success without pain, almost without effort except of a pleasurable kind, success accompanied by moral and esthetic beauty, as well as the most desirable material reward. Wealth, naturally, could not be an end in itself: alone, it was not Success. But it was the unobtrusive companion of all true Success. . . . From this point of view he was cheerfully explicit about Carlos. Carlos had always been contemptuous of the Eternal Laws. He had always simply written his tunes without giving a thought to the profounder inferences of music, based as it is upon the harmonic system of the spheres. . . . He, Betancourt, had many times warned Carlos. It had done no good at all. Carlos had gone on inviting his own doom.

"I have warned you, too," he said to me kindly. "I have asked myself many times why you will not or cannot accept the Mysteries which would open a whole treasure house for you. . . . All," he said, "is possible through scientific intuition. If you depend on mere intellect, you must fail."

"You must fail," he had been saying all this time to poor simple Carlos. "He has failed," he said of him to others. He now looked almost fondly upon his handiwork, who sat there, somewhat grubby and gloomy, a man who had done a good day's work in his time, and was not altogether finished yet. The neat light figure beside me posed gracefully upon its slender spine, the too-beautiful slender hands waved rhythmically upon insubstantial wrists. I remembered all that Carlos had done for Betancourt in other days; he had, in his thoughtless hopelessly human way, piled upon these thin shoulders a greater burden of gratitude than they could support. Betancourt had set in motion all the machinery of the laws of Universal Harmony he could command to help him revenge himself on Carlos. It was slow work, but he never tired.

"I don't, of course, understand just what you mean by failure, or by success either," I told him at last. "You know, I never could understand."

"It is true, you could not," he said, "that was the great trouble."

"As for Carlos," I said, "you should forgive him. . . ."

Betancourt said with perfect sincerity, "You know I never blame anyone for anything at all."

Carlos came round and shook hands with me as everybody pushed back his chair and began drifting out by the several doorways. He was full of humanity and good humor about Justino and his troubles. "These family love affairs," he said, "what can you expect?"

"Oh, no, now," said Betancourt, uneasily. He laughed his twanging tremulous little laugh.

"Oh, yes, now," said Carlos, walking beside me. "I shall make a *corrido* about Justino and his sister." He began to sing almost in a whisper, imitating the voice and gestures of a singer peddling broadsides in the market. . . . *Ah, poor little Rosalita*
Took herself a new lover,
Thus betraying the heart's core
Of her impassioned brother. . . .

266

Now she lies dead, poor Rosalita,
With two bullets in her heart. . . .
Take warning, my young sisters,
Who would from your brothers part.

"One bullet," said Betancourt, wagging a long finger at Carlos. "One bullet!"

Carlos laughed. "Very well, one bullet! Such a precisionist! Good night," he said.

Kennerly and Carlos disappeared early. Don Genaro spent the evening playing billiards with Stepanov, who won always. Don Genaro was very good at billiards, but Stepanov was a champion, with all sorts of trophies to show, so it was no humiliation to be defeated by him.

In the drafty upper-hall room fitted up as a parlor, Andreyev turned off the mechanical attachment of the piano and sang Russian songs, running his hands over the keys while he waited to remember yet other songs. Doña Julia and I sat listening. He sang for us, but for himself mostly, in the same kind of voluntary forgetfulness of his surroundings, the same self-induced absence of mind that had kept him talking about Russia in the afternoon.

We sat until very late. Doña Julia smiled steadily every time she caught the glance of Andreyev or myself, yawning now and then under her hand, her Pekinese sprawling and snoring on her lap. "You're not tired?" I asked her. "You wouldn't let us stay up too late?"

"Oh, no, let's go on with the music. I love sitting up all night. I never go to bed if I can possibly sit up. Don't go yet."

At half-past one Uspensky sent for Andreyev, for Stepanov. He was restless, in a fever, he wished to talk. Andreyev said, "I have already sent for Doctor Volk. It is better not to delay."

Doña Julia and I looked on in the billiard room downstairs, where Stepanov and don Genaro were settling the score. Several Indians leaned in at the windows, their vast straw hats tilted forward, watching in silence. Doña Julia asked her husband, "Then you're not going to Mexico tonight?"

"Why should I?" he inquired sullenly without looking at her.

"I thought you might," said doña Julia. "Good night, Stepanov," she said, her black eyes shining under her long lids painted silver blue.

"Good night, Julita," said Stepanov, his frank Northern smile meaning anything or nothing at all. When he was not smiling, his face was severe, expressive, and intensely alive. His smile was misleadingly simple, like a very young boy's. He was anything but simple; he smiled now like a merry open book upon the absurd

268

little figure strayed out of a marionette theater. Turning away, doña Julia slanted at him the glittering eye of a femme fatale in any Hollywood film. He examined the end of his cue as if he looked through a microscope. Don Genaro said violently, "Good night!" and disappeared violently through the door leading to the corral.

Doña Julia and I passed through her apartment, a long shallow room between the billiard and the vat-room. It was puffy with silk and down, glossy with bright new polished wood and wide mirrors, restless with small ornaments, boxes of sweets, French dolls in ruffled skirts and white wigs. The air was thick with perfume which fought with another heavier smell. From the vat-room came a continual muffled shouting, the rumble of barrels as they rolled down the wooden trestles to the flat mule-car standing on the tracks running past the wide doorway. The smell had not been out of my nostrils since I came, but here it rose in a thick vapor through the heavy drone of flies, sour, stale, like rotting milk and blood; this sound and this smell belonged together, and both belonged to the intermittent rumble of barrels and the long chanting cry of the Indians. On the narrow stairs I glanced back at doña Julia. She was looking up, wrinkling her little nose, her Pekinese with his wrinkled nose of perpetual disgust held close to her face. "Pulque!" she said. "Isn't it horrid? But I hope the noise will not keep you awake."

On my balcony there was no longer any perfume to disturb the keen fine wind from the mountains, or the smell from the vat-room. "Twenty-one!" sang the Indians in a long, melodious chorus of weariness and excitement, and the twenty-first barrel of fresh pulque rolled down the slide, was seized by two men and loaded on the flat-car under my window.

From the window next to mine, the three Russian voices murmured along quietly. Pigs grunted and rooted in the soft wallow near the washing fountain, where the women were still kneeling in the darkness, thumping wet cloth on the stones, chattering, laughing. All the women seemed to be laughing that night: long after midnight, the high bright sound sparkled again and again from the long row of peon quarters along the corral. Burros sobbed and mourned to each other, there was everywhere the drowsy wakefulness of creatures, stamping hoofs, breathing and snorting. Below in the vat-room a single voice sang suddenly a dozen notes of some rowdy song; and the women at the washing fountain were silenced for a moment, then tittered among themselves. There occurred a light flurry at the arch of the gate leading into the inner patio: one of the polite, expensive dogs had lost his dignity and was chasing, with snarls of real annoyance, a little fat-bottomed soldier back to his proper place, the barracks by the wall opposite the Indian huts. The soldier scrambled and stumbled silently away, without resistance, his dim lantern agitated violently. At a certain point, as if here was the invisible boundary line, the dog stopped, watched while the soldier ran on, then returned to his post under the archway. The soldiers, sent by the government as a guard against the Agrarians, sprawled in idleness eating their beans at don Genaro's expense. He tolerated and resented them, and so did the dogs.

I fell asleep to the long chanting of the Indians, counting their barrels in the vat-room, and woke again at sunrise, summer sunrise, to their long doleful morning song, the clatter of metal and hard leather, and the stamping of mules as they were being harnessed to the flat-cars. . . . The drivers swung their whips and shouted, the loaded cars creaked and slid away in a procession, off to meet the pulque train for Mexico City. The field workers were leaving for the maguey fields, driving their donkeys. They shouted, too, and whacked the donkeys with sticks, but no one was really hurrying, nor really excited. It was just another day's work, another day's weariness. A three-year-old man-child ran beside his father; he drove a weanling donkey carrying two miniature casks on its furry back. The two small creatures imitated each in his own kind perfectly the gestures of their elders. The baby whacked and shouted, the donkey trudged and flapped his ears at each blow.

"My God!" said Kennerly over coffee an hour later. "Do you remember—" he beat off a cloud of flies and filled his cup with a wobbling hand—"I thought of it all night and couldn't sleep—*don't* you remember," he implored Stepanov, who held one palm over his coffee cup while he finished a cigarette, "those scenes we shot only two weeks ago, when Justino played the part of a boy who killed a girl by accident, tried to escape, and Vicente was one of the men who ran him down on horseback? Well, the same thing has happened to the same people in *reality!* And—" he turned to me, "the strangest thing is, we have to make that scene again, it didn't turn out so well, and look, my God, we had it happening really, and nobody thought of it then! Then was the time. We could have got a close-up of the girl, really dead, and real blood running down Justino's face where Vicente hit him, and my God! we never even thought of it. That kind of thing," he said, bitterly, "has been happening ever since we got here. Just happens over and over. . . . Now, what was the matter, I wonder?"

He stared at Stepanov full of accusation. Stepanov lifted his palm from his cup, and beating off flies, drank. "Light no good, probably," he said. His eyes flickered open, clicked shut in Kennerly's direction, as if they had taken a snapshot of something and that episode was finished.

"If you want to look at it that way," said Kennerly, with resentment, "but after all, there it was, it had happened, it wasn't our fault, and we might as well have had it."

"We can always do it again," said Stepanov. "When Justino comes back, and the light is better. The light," he said to me, "it is always our enemy. Here we have one good day in five, or less."

"Imagine," said Kennerly, pouncing, "just try to imagine that—when that poor boy comes back he'll have to go through the same scene he has gone through twice before, once in play and once in reality. *Reality!*" He licked his chops. "Think how he'll feel. Why, it ought to drive him crazy."

"If he comes back," said Stepanov, "we must think of that."

In the patio half a dozen Indian boys, their ragged white clothes exposing their tawny smooth skin, were flinging over the sleek-backed horses great saddles of deerskin encrusted with silver embroidery and mother-of-pearl. The women were returning to the washing fountain. The pigs were out rooting in their favorite wallows, and in the vat-room, silently, the day-workers were already filling the bullhide vats with freshly drawn pulque juice. Carlos Montaña was out early too, enjoying himself in the fresh morning air, watching three dogs chase a long-legged pig from wallow to barn. The pig, screaming steadily, galloped like a rocking horse towards the known safety of his pen, the dogs nipping at his heels just enough to keep him up to his best speed. Carlos roared with joy, holding his ribs, and the Indian boys laughed with him.

The Spanish overseer, who had been cast for the rôle of villain—one of them—in the film, came out wearing a new pair of tight riding trousers, of deerskin and silver embroidery, like the saddles, and sat slouched on the long bench near the arch, facing the great corral where the Indians and soldiers were. There he sat nearly all day, as he had sat for years and might sit for years more. His long wry North-Spanish face was dead with boredom. He slouched, with his English cap pulled over his close-set eyes, and did not even glance to see what Carlos was laughing at. Andreyev and I waved to Carlos and he came over at once. He was still laughing. It seemed he had forgotten the pig and was laughing at the overseer, who had already forty pairs of fancy charro trousers, but had thought none of them quite good enough for the film and had caused to be made, at great expense, the pair he was now wearing, which were entirely too tight. He hoped by wearing them every day to stretch them. He was miserable, entirely, for his trousers were all he had to live for, anyhow. "All he can do with his life," said Andreyev, "is to put on a different pair of fancy trousers every day, and sit on that bench hoping that something, anything, may happen."

I said I should have thought there had been enough happening for the past few weeks . . . or at any rate the past few days.

"Oh, no," said Carlos, "nothing that lasts long enough. I mean real excitement like the last Agrarian raid. . . . There were machine guns on the towers, and every man on the place had a rifle and a pistol. They had the time of their lives. They drove the raiders off, and then they fired the rest of their ammunition in the air by way of celebration; and the next day they were bored. They wanted to have the whole show over again. It was very hard to explain to them that the fiesta was ended."

"They do really hate the Agrarians, then?" I asked.

"No, they love excitement," said Carlos.

We walked through the vat-room, picking our way through the puddles of sap sinking into the mud floor, idly stopping to watch, without comment, the flies drowning in the stinking liquor which seeped over the hairy bullhides sagging between the wooden frames. María Santísima stood primly in her blue painted niche in a frame of fly-blown paper flowers, with a perpetual light at her feet. The walls were covered with a faded fresco relating the legend of pulque; how a young Indian girl discovered this divine liquor, and brought it to the emperor, who rewarded her well; and after her death she became a half-goddess. An old legend: maybe the oldest: something to do with man's confused veneration for, and terror of, the fertility of women and vegetation. . . .

Betancourt stood in the door sniffing the air bravely. He glanced around the walls with the eye of an expert. "This is a very good example," he said, smiling at the fresco, "the perfect example, really. . . . The older ones are always the best, of course. It is a fact," he said, "that the Spaniards found wall paintings in the pre-Conquest pulquerías . . . always telling this legend. So it goes on. Nothing ever ends," he waved his long beautiful hand, "it goes on being and becomes little by little something else."

"I'd call that an end, of a kind," said Carlos.

"Oh, well, *you*," said Betancourt, smiling with immense indulgence upon his old friend, who was becoming gradually something else.

At ten o'clock don Genaro emerged on his way to visit the village judge once more. Doña Julia, Andreyev, Stepanov, Carlos, and I were walking on the roofs in the intermittent sun-and-cloud light, looking out over the immense landscape of patterned field and mountain. Stepanov carried his small camera and took snapshots of us, with the dogs. We had already had our pictures taken on the steps with a nursling burro, with Indian babies; at the fountain on the long upper terrace to the south, where the grandfather lived; before the closed chapel door (with Carlos being a fat pious priest); in the patio still farther back with the ruins of the old monastery stone bath; and in the pulquería.

So we were tired of snapshots, and leaned in a row over the roof to watch don Genaro take his leave. . . . He leaped down the shallow steps with half a dozen Indian boys standing back for him to pass, hurled himself at the saddle of his Arab mare, his man let go the bridle instantly and leaped to his own horse, and don Genaro rode hell-for-leather out of the corral with his mounted man pounding twenty feet behind him. Dogs, pigs, burros, women, babies, boys, chickens, scattered and fled before him, little soldiers hurled back the great outer gates at his approach, and the two went through at a dead run, disappearing into the hollow of the road. . . .

"That judge will never let Justino go without the money, I know that, and everybody knows it. Genaro knows it. Yet he will still go and fight and fight," said doña Julia in her toneless soft voice, without rebuke.

"Oh, it is barely possible he may," said Carlos. "If Velarde sends word, you'll see—Justino will pop out! like that!" He shot an imaginary pea between forefinger and thumb.

"Yes, but think how Genaro will have to pay Velarde!" said doña Julia. "It's too tiresome, just when the film was going so well." She looked at Stepanov.

He said, "Stay just that way one little second," raised his camera and pressed the lever; then turned, gazed through the lens at a figure standing in the lower patio. Foreshortened, dirty gray-white against dirty yellow-gray wall, hat pulled down over his eyes, arms folded, Vicente stood without moving. He had been standing there for some time, staring. At last he did move; walked away suddenly with some decision, almost to the gate; then stood again staring, framed in the archway. Stepanov took another picture of him.

I said, to Andreyev, walking a little apart, "I wonder why he did not let his friend Justino escape, or at least give him his chance to try. . . . Why did he go after him, I wonder?"

"Revenge," said Andreyev. "Imagine a man's friend

betraying him so, and with a woman, and a sister! He was furious. He did not know what he was doing, maybe. . . . Now I imagine he is regretting it."

In two hours don Genaro and his servant were back; they approached the hacienda at a reasonable pace, but once fairly in sight they whipped up their horses and charged into the corral in the same style as when they left it. The servants, suddenly awake, ran back and forth, up and down steps, round and round; the animals scurried for refuge as before. Three Indian boys flew to the mare's bridle, but Vicente was first. He leaped and danced as the mare plunged and fought for her head, his eyes fixed on don Genaro, who flung himself to the ground, landed lightly as an acrobat, and strode away with a perfectly expressionless face.

Nothing had happened. The judge still wanted two thousand pesos to let Justino go. This may have been the answer Vicente expected. He sat against the wall all afternoon, knees drawn up to his chin, hat over his eyes, his feet in their ragged sandals fallen limp on their sides. In half an hour the evil news was known even to the farthest man in the maguey fields. At the table, don Genaro ate and drank in silent haste, like a man who must catch the last train for a journey on which his life depends. "No, I won't have this," he broke out, hammering the table beside his plate. "Do you know what that imbecile judge said to me? He asked me why I worried so much over one peon. I told him it was my business what I chose to worry about. He said he had heard we were making a picture over here with men shooting each other in it. He said he had a jailful of men waiting to be shot, and he'd be glad to send them over for us to shoot in the picture. He couldn't see why, he said, we were pretending to kill people when we could have all we needed to kill really. He thinks Justino should be shot, too. Let him try it! But never in this world will I give him two thousand pesos!"

At sunset the men driving the burros came in from the maguey fields. The workers in the vat-room began to empty the fermented pulque into barrels, and to pour the fresh maguey water into the reeking bullhide vats. The chanting and counting and the rolling of barrels down the incline began again for the night. The white flood of pulque flowed without pause; all over Mexico the Indians would drink the corpse-white liquor, swallow forgetfulness and ease by the riverful, and the money would flow silver-white into the government treasury; don Genaro and his fellow-hacendados would fret and curse, the Agrarians would raid, and ambitious politicians in the capital would be stealing right and left enough to buy such haciendas for themselves. It was all arranged.

We spent the evening in the billiard room. Doctor Volk had arrived, had passed an hour with Uspensky, who had a simple sore throat and a threat of tonsilitis. Doctor Volk would cure him. Meantime he played a round of billiards with Stepanov and don Genaro. He was a splendid, conscientious, hard-working doctor, a Russian, and he could not conceal his delight at being once more with Russians, having a little holiday with a patient who was not very sick, after all, and a chance to play billiards, which he loved. When it was his turn, he climbed, smiling, on the edge of the table, leaned halfway down the green baize, closed one eye, balanced his cue and sighted and balanced again. Without taking his shot, he rolled off the table, smiling, placed himself at another angle, sighted again, leaned over almost flat, sighted, took his shot, and missed, smiling. Then it was Stepanov's turn. "I simply cannot understand it," said Doctor Volk, shaking his head, watching Stepanov with such an intensity of admiration that his eyes watered.

Andreyev sat on a low stool playing the guitar and singing Russian songs in a continuous murmur. Doña Julia curled up on the divan near him, in her black pajamas, with her Pekinese slung around her neck like a scarf. The beast snuffled and groaned and rolled his eyes in a swoon of flabby enjoyment. The big dogs sniffed around him with pained knotted foreheads. He yammered and snapped and whimpered at them. "They cannot believe he is really a dog," said doña Julia in delight. Carlos and Betancourt sat at a small table with music and costume designs spread before them. They were talking as if they were going over again a subject which wearied them both. . . .

I was learning a new card game with a thin dark youth who was some sort of assistant to Betancourt. He was very sleek and slim-waisted and devoted, he said, to fresco painting, "only modern," he told me, "like Rivera's, the method, but not old-fashioned style like his. I am decorating a house in Cuernavaca, come and look at it. You will see what I mean. You should not have played the dagger," he added; "now I shall play the crown, and there you are, defeated." He gathered up the cards and shuffled them. "When Justino was here," he said, "the director was always having trouble with him in the serious scenes, because Justino thought everything was a joke. In the death scenes, he smiled all over his face and ruined a great deal of film. Now they are saying that when Justino comes back no one will ever have to say again to him, 'Don't laugh, Justino, this is death, this is not funny.'"

Doña Julia turned her Pekinese over and rolled him

back and forth on her lap. "He will forget everything, the minute it is over . . . his sister, everything," she said, gently, looking at me with soft empty eyes. "They are animals. Nothing means anything to them. And," she added, "it is quite possible he may not come back."

A silence like a light trance fell over the whole room in which all these chance-gathered people who had nothing to say to each other were for the moment imprisoned. Action was their defense against the predicament they were in, all together, and for the moment nothing was happening. The suspense in the air seemed ready to explode when Kennerly came in almost on tiptoe, like a man entering church. Everybody turned toward him as if he were in himself a whole rescue party. He announced his bad news loudly: "I've got to go back to Mexico City tonight. There's all sorts of trouble there. About the film. I better get back there and have it out with the censors. I just talked over the telephone there and he says there is some talk about cutting out a whole reel . . . you know, that scene with the beggars at the fiesta."

Don Genaro laid down his cue. "I'm going back tonight," he said; "you can go with me."

"Tonight?" doña Julia turned her face towards him, her eyes down. "What for?"

"Lolita," he said briefly and angrily. "She must come

back. They have to make three or four scenes over again."

"Ah, that's lovely!" said doña Julia. She buried her face in the fur of her little dog. "Ah, lovely! Lolita back again! Do go for her—I can't wait!"

Stepanov spoke over his shoulder to Kennerly with no attempt to conceal his impatience—"I shouldn't worry about the censors—let them have their way!"

Kennerly's jaw jerked and his voice trembled: "My God! I've *got* to worry and *somebody* has got to think of the future around here!"

Ten minutes later don Genaro's powerful car roared past the billiard room and fled down the wild dark road towards the capital.

In the morning there began a gradual drift back to town, by train, by automobile. "Stay here," each said to me in turn, "we are coming back tomorrow, Uspensky will be feeling better, the work will begin again." Doña Julia was stopping in bed. I said good-by to her in the afternoon. She was sleepy and downy, curled up with her Pekinese on her shoulder. "Tomorrow," she said, "Lolita will be here, and there will be great excitement. They are going to do some of the best scenes over again." I could not wait for tomorrow in this deathly air. "If you should come back in about ten days," said the Indian driver, "you would see a different place. It is very sad here now. But then the green corn will be ready, and ah, there will be enough to eat again!"